KENT P. EGGING

THE GOD WHO CARES
A Christian Looks at Judaism

THE GOD
WHO CARES

A Christian looks at Judaism

by

FREDRICK HOLMGREN

JOHN KNOX PRESS
ATLANTA

Library of Congress Cataloging in Publication Data

Holmgren, Fredrick, 1926–
  The God who cares.

  Includes bibliographies.
    1. Judaism. 2. Christianity and other
religions—Judaism. 3. Judaism—Relations—
Christianity. I. Title.
BM565.H64   296   78-52445
ISBN 0-8042-0588-4

© copyright 1979 John Knox Press
Printed in the United States of America
Atlanta, Georgia

To
Betty
Margaret
Mark

PREFACE

This volume is addressed to Christians who are unfamiliar with the teachings of Judaism. It reflects the work of both Jewish and Christian scholars, but it is a nontechnical presentation of some central themes in ancient and modern Judaism. The book has in mind the layperson and student, but it also addresses the pastor who was given only a cursory introduction to Judaism in seminary.

Although the discussion in the book covers several aspects of Jewish thought, the focus is on Law and Love. Generally, Christians are not well informed in these areas. Misconception of these basic beliefs in the Jewish tradition keeps alive the old caricatures of Judaism and prevents genuine dialogue between Jews and Christians. To promote understanding of these themes the following pages direct attention to the witness of ancient and modern Jewish literature.

Chapter One contains a brief summary of Jewish-Christian relationships from the New Testament period to the twentieth century. The next three chapters concern themselves with the understanding of Law, Mercy, and Sacrifice in the Hebrew Bible. Chapter Five explores early Jewish writings which are a mystery to most Christians. In Chapters Six and Seven, the teachings of Law and Love are considered in the light of selected rabbinic passages. The Pharisees, long viewed as legalistic interpreters of the Law, are the subject of inquiry in Chapter Eight. An investigation of the nature of Law in modern Judaism is undertaken in Chapter Nine by means of a discussion of the thought of Abraham Joshua Heschel. The final chapter points up a two-fold problem in the Jewish-Christian relationship: the Christian is tempted to caricature Judaism as a sterile, legalistic religion and to idealize the contribution that Christian faith makes to life.

A sabbatical leave, during the academic year of 1975–76, provided the leisure necessary for the research and writing of this volume. I am grateful to North Park Theological Seminary for granting me this "free time." Through the generosity of Mr. Robert S. Adler and Mr. Charles F. Sebastian, I was able to spend part of my sabbatical as a Visiting Scholar at Hebrew Union College-Jewish Institute of Religion in Cincinnati, Ohio. There I enjoyed the courtesy of the faculty and student community as well as the friendly cooperation of the Dean of Graduate Studies, Dr. Samuel Sandmel. Also, I remember with pleasure my acquaintance with Professors Ellis Rivkin and Michael Cook, whose lectures in Pharisaism and Rabbinic Literature respectively, stimulated my own research in this area. In addition, I am indebted to Dr. Cook for reading the chapter on the Pharisees and making helpful comments.

Special appreciation is due Dr. Byron Sherwin, Spertus College of Judaica in Chicago, who has read a major portion of this work and offered valued suggestions for its improvement. Also Dr. Elder Lindahl's discerning critique of the manuscript has initiated a number of revisions in the text. Further, I appreciate the encouragement and wise counsel given me by Dr. Richard Ray, Director, John Knox Press. Other friends and colleagues, for whose interest and advice I am thankful, are: James Alger, Glenn Anderson, Solomon Bernards, Jonathan Collins, William Bruce, David Hawkinson, F. Burton Nelson, Elmer Ost, Klyne Snodgrass, and James Widboom.

I am grateful for the life and scholarship of Nils W. Lund, former Dean of North Park Theological Seminary. Not only did he introduce me to the Hebrew Scriptures, he passed on an appreciation of the Jewish tradition which further matured under the teaching of W. D. Davies and F. C. Grant at Union

Theological Seminary in New York. The influence of Dr. Lund's successor, Dean Emeritus Eric G. Hawkinson, is present still. His generous spirit and careful listening to the words of others has served as a model for many students. Finally a word of appreciation to Mr. Robert Collins of Chappaqua, New York, for his friendship and continuing interest in my work. Although my debt to the persons named above is considerable, I alone am responsible for the final form of this volume.

Fredrick Holmgren

Table of Contents

Preface

Introduction   A New Era for Jews and Christians   13

Chapter One   Past Jewish-Christian Relationships   17

Chapter Two   Old Testament Law, a Divine Gift   32

Chapter Three   The Righteous Mercy of God in the Old
Testament   44

Chapter Four   Sacrifice, a Symbol of Inner Commitment   53

Chapter Five   The Early Literature of Judaism   63

Chapter Six   Jewish Teaching on the Law   69

Chapter Seven   Jewish Teaching on the Love of God   77

Chapter Eight   The Pharisees and Jesus   85

Chapter Nine   The Character of Modern Judaism   107

Chapter Ten   A Christian Approach to Judaism   130

Introduction

A NEW ERA
FOR
JEWS AND CHRISTIANS

"BUT THE TIME HAS COME!"

The above phrase is taken from a communication[1] sent to the Christian Churches of Chicago by Rabbi Gerson B. Levi, President of the Chicago Rabbinical Association and Editor of the *Reform Advocate*. The letter conveyed "hearty greetings to Christians . . . upon the gladsome festival of Christmas." In calling for better relationships between the Church and Synagogue, Rabbi Levi noted the many areas in which there is basic agreement. He also observed that the two communities differed on significant issues but, declared: "The time has come when, across these differences, the hand of good will should be extended ungrudgingly and heartily." The year was 1929!

SINCE 1929

Rabbi Levi's letter was written on the eve of Hitler's war against the Jews. His friendly, generous communication seeking understanding and goodwill contrasts sharply with the hate that began the Great Persecution under the Nazis. It was not the time for better Jewish-Christian relationships. Has the time come now? Maybe. In the present day, Jews and Christians *are* reaching out to each other. The long period of estrangement, characterized by indifference and hostility, *may be* yielding to a new spirit in the world. The two communities are beginning to confront each other with friendly firmness. Not only are points of agreement affirmed, but areas of tension are acknowledged and discussed. Not everyone in the Jewish and Christian communities is involved in this confrontation, but a growing number of people in the Church and Synagogue are beginning to talk *with,* instead of *at,* each other. Jews and Christians appear to be listening to what the partner in the conversation is saying. This is a sign of hope. Perhaps "the time has come" —finally.

DISPUTATION OR DIALOGUE?

One of the problems in past Jewish-Christian encounters is that the participants have been too eager to defend the teachings of their own faith. From a "fighting stance" few people are able to listen carefully to the words of the "opponent." No wonder Judaism is misrepresented in Christian circles and Christianity takes on a strange character among Jews.

Because we always look at the religion of another as an "outsider," we do not see or experience the inner life of that faith. Christians can never understand Judaism as fully as can the Jewish "insider." Nor can a Jew appreciate Christianity as does a Christian. Nevertheless, we can learn to listen to what adherents of the other religion say about their faith and then, to the best of our ability, accurately express what is being said.

OTHERWORLDLY CHRISTIANS—LEGALISTIC JEWS?

Christians rightfully object when Jewish interpreters describe Christianity as an "other-worldly" religion, which has only minimal concern for this world and the problems of people who live in it. Christian "insiders" know that this is an unfair representation of Christianity. Yet, if an "outsider" looks at some passages in the New Testament and reads the writings of certain preachers and theologians, Christianity may seem to be concerned only about souls and heaven. Emphasis on the other world *is* present in Christian thought. Sometimes it has received undue stress. When viewed in isolation from other aspects of Christian theology or life, a distorted picture of Christianity emerges.

Jews are disturbed also when Christians speak about the lifeless, unsatisfying legalism of Judaism. Although an "outsider" may find support for such a judgment in some passages of the Talmud and other Jewish writings, it is basically a false characterization of this age old religion. "You can find whatever you want in the Bible," so goes the saying. True! The same may be said about the Talmud and other rabbinic literature from which Judaism draws its life. The biblical and rabbinic writings are a vast literature. They contain many and varied teachings. Some are more admirable than others. There *are* "problem" passages in the Old Testament and later Jewish literature (they exist in the New Testament also), but they do not appear to represent the central concerns of the Jewish community. If Judaism is to be considered, let her be examined in terms of those views that are at the core of her faith, not by those that exist on the periphery. As a Christian I hope that Christianity will be appraised in this same fashion.

NOTES

1. See *The Covenant Companion* 8 (January 9, 1929) p. 3.

Chapter One

PAST JEWISH-CHRISTIAN RELATIONSHIPS

DISAGREEMENT

Jews and Christians have lived together for over nineteen hundred years; yet, even today, Christians know very little about Judaism. What is "known" is too often a distorted form of Jewish teaching. A striking phenomenon, when one considers that not only do Jews and Christians share the same Scripture, but the New Testament reflects both the teachings of the Old Testament and post-biblical Jewish literature. No doubt the very closeness of the two faiths accounts, in large measure, for the distance and tension between them. While the Old Testament represents a common ground, Christianity interpreted this Scripture quite differently than did Judaism. The hostility which accompanied this disagreement may be seen already in the writings of the New Testament. This literature recounts the conflict between the Pharisees and Jesus, as well as the persecution of the early Christians by members of the Jewish community. The sharp language used by some New Testament writers also reveals the tension between the two communities. The following passage in 1 Thessalonians 2:15 does not represent one who is carefully measuring his speech. On the contrary, these are angry words spoken in the midst of conflict. The Jews are those who killed both the Lord Jesus and the prophets, and drove us out, and displease God and oppose all men by hindering us from speaking to the Gentiles that they may be saved—so as always to fill up the measure of their sins. But God's wrath has come upon them at last!

The same animosity is evident in the Gospel of John, where it is said of the Jews: " 'You are of your father the devil, and your will is to do your father's desires.' " (8:44)

OPPOSITION

The antagonism to Judaism, already present in the New Testament, became fierce, and even savage, opposition in the tracts and sermons of the Church Fathers. They looked upon the Jews as condemned by their own Scriptures. The prophets' denunciations of Israel were read as if nearly all Israelites were guilty of evil. The Fathers considered them to be an unusually wicked people. No one recognized that the prophets frequently used exaggerated speech to make their point. What appears in their oracles to be a condemnation of everyone, amounts in reality to a censure of some. Further, none of the Fathers expressed any surprise that these "very wicked Jews" preserved the Old Testament as Scripture, even though it was critical of many aspects of Israelite life. No one asked: "Does an evil nation retain as Scripture those writings that burn its ears?" Also, the Fathers of the Church ignored the fact that the basic charges of the prophets could be leveled against the Christian community of their time—and of every time.

CURSED JEWS, BLESSED CHRISTIANS

A strange exegesis of the Old Testament was employed in the Church to mark the Jews as a condemned people before God. The prophetic writings, containing both threats

and promises, are addressed to Israelites. However, early
Christian interpreters assigned the accusations and threats to
the Jews and reserved the promises of peace to the Christian
Church, which emerged hundreds of years after the appearance of the prophets. Curses are for Jews, blessings for
Christians! The great men of faith in the Old Testament
were claimed by the Church, while the rebellious sinners of
old Israel were identified as the forefathers of the Jews. The
Church was considered to be without blemish and the Synagogue without virtue. Nothing was too bad to say about the
Jews, as may be seen from the writings of some prominent
early Christians.

NOTHING TOO BAD TO SAY

Chrysostom, "the golden mouthed orator" (344-407) was the
most venomous of the Church Fathers when it came to Jews.

"As an animal, when it has been fattened by getting all it wants
to eat, gets stubborn and hard to manage, so it was with the Jewish
people. Reduced by gluttony and drunkenness to a state of utter
depravity, they frisked about and would not accept Christ's yoke."

"If someone had killed your son, could you stand the sight of him
or the sound of his greeting? Wouldn't you try to get away from
him as if he were an evil demon; as if he were the Devil himself?
The Jews killed the Son of your Master. . . . Will you so dishonor
Him as to respect and cultivate His Murderers, the men who
crucified Him?"[1]

"But it was men, says the Jew, who brought these misfortunes
upon us, not God. On the contrary, it was in fact God who
brought them about. . . . Men would certainly not have made war
unless God had permitted them. . . . Is it not obvious that it was
because [God] hated you and rejected you once for all?"[2]

Other Church Fathers also vented considerable anger
against the Jewish community. Harsh words moved readily to
the lips of Hippolytus (170-236):

"It is because you killed Christ. It is because you stretched out your hand against the Lord. It is because you shed the precious blood, that there is now no restoration, no mercy anymore and no defense. . . . But now you have eclipsed everything in the past and through your madness against Christ, you have committed the ultimate transgression. This is why you are being punished worse now than in the past."[3]

Gregory of Nyssa (331-396) called up the following phrases to describe the Jews:

"Slayers of the Lord, murderers of the prophets, adversaries of God, . . . men who show contempt for the law, foes of grace, enemies of their father's faith, advocates of the devil, brood of vipers, slanderers, scoffers, men whose minds are in darkness, leaven of the Pharisees, assembly of demons, sinners, wicked men, stoners, and haters of righteousness.'"[4]

JEWISH RITUALS UNDER ATTACK

Not only were the Jews themselves looked upon as unusually wicked persons, but their religious rituals came under attack also. In the Epistle of Diognetus (3rd century), it is said that the sacrifices of the Jews " 'are absurd . . . their scruples about the Sabbath ridiculous, their vaunting of circumcision nonsense, and their festivals folly.' "[5] John Chrysostom, who never was an advocate of restraint, likens the Synagogue to a whorehouse. Commenting on Jeremiah 3:3 he declares: " 'But the place where the harlot is prostituted is the brothel. The synagogue therefore is not only a theater, it is a place of prostitution, it is a den of thieves and a hiding-place of wild animals.' "[6] Chrysostom also suggested that God never fully approved of sacrifice but "gave in" to the Jews' mad desire for it.

And this is what God did. He saw the Jews raving mad, choking themselves in their lust for sacrifices, and ready if they didn't get them to desert to idolatry . . . or rather, not ready to do so, but already doing so. Then it was that he permitted the sacrifices.[7]

Likewise, circumcision came under the critical eye of Christian theologians. Justin Martyr (2nd century), in his "dialogue" with Trypho, argues that it was a sign of God's disapproval, for it

> "was given for a sign, that you should be separated from other nations and us [i.e., Christians], and that you alone should rightly suffer the things you suffer now, and that your lands should be desolate and your cities burned with fire, and that foreigners should eat up the fruits before your face, and none of you go up to Jerusalem. . . ."[8]

Concerning the establishment of the Sabbath, John of Damascus (8th century) declared that it was ordained as a day of rest, so that there would be at least one day in seven when the Jews would not be able to seek material gain for themselves:

> At any rate, to start with the inferior and grosser things, as my unlearned self understands it, when God saw the grossness and sensuality of the people of Israel and their absolute propensity for material things, as well as their indiscretion, then first of all He prescribed that "the manservant and ox should rest."[9]

A number of Church Fathers mounted an attack on the Mosaic Law itself. They attempted to demonstrate that it could not give life, and that it did not reflect God's will for humankind. Ignoring the many passages which affirm that the Law is good and a gift from God, the Fathers quoted (out of context) the following passage from Ezekiel 20:25: "Moreover I gave them statutes that were not good and ordinances by which they could not have life."[10]

KILLING GOD

Although there were Christian laypersons, priests, rulers, and Popes who showed kindness to the Jews, the prevailing view in the Church considered them to be a people in rebellion against God. They had, so it was believed, committed horrendous sins for centuries, but this depravity culminated in the crime above all crimes, namely, the murder of Jesus, the Son of God. For this act the Jews were accused of committing deicide—the killing of God! Only in the Second Vatican Council of 1965 was this charge repudiated, although not without some equivocation.

THE CRIMES OF THE JEWS

The Jews were not only thought to be in rebellion against God, they were regarded as in league with the devil. It was rather common in medieval art and literature to portray the Jews with horns and a tail. These "demonic" people who had the ear of the devil himself, were accused of a variety of crimes, for example: murder, kidnapping, practicing magic, seduction of Christian women, poisoning wells, and stealing the bread used in the celebration of the Eucharist. Also some people thought that the Jews were the cause of earthquakes, storms, and plagues![11] Some of their crimes are detailed in the following proclamations of two thirteenth century Popes. The Jews, declares Gregory IX

"kidnap Christian boys, and steal whatever else they can, and sell them to the Saracens. Nor are they afraid to commit other enormities likewise in injury of the Christian name and the scandalization and ruin of many. Wherefore, since, in order that evils of this sort might be the more easily and completely avoided, the General Council decided after careful deliberation, that Jews of either sex shall in all Christian lands and at all times be distinguished from Christians by the nature of their clothes."[12]

Innocent IV denounces the Jews of his day whom the Church has allowed to live among Christians despite the enormity of their sins. But, even though the Christian community has given this kind of "consideration" to the Jews, they do not change. They continue their perverse ways. Not only do they reject Jesus Christ, they "despise the Law of Moses and the prophets, and follow some tradition of their elders. . . . In traditions of this sort they rear and nurture their children, which traditions, are called Talmud in Hebrew. It is a big book among them, exceeding in size the text of the Bible. In it are found blasphemies against God and His Christ, and obviously entangled fables about the Blessed Virgin, and abusive errors, and unheard follies. But of the laws and doctrines of the prophets they make their sons altogether ignorant."[13]

"CRUEL AND UNUSUAL PUNISHMENT"

A proclamation by Innocent IV in 1247, which desires to bring about a more humane relationship between Christians and Jews, further illustrates the barbarous treatment of Jewish people by the Christian populace. The Pope reminds the followers of Christ that it is both inhuman and unchristian to oppress the Jews as they have done. He then refers to a petition sent him by the Jews of a province in France, who had been

"accused of having nailed to the cross a certain girl who had been found dead in a certain ditch, though they were not convicted, nor had they confessed, nor had they even been accused by anyone, the noble Draconet, lord of Montauban in the diocese of Vaison, despoiled them of all their goods and cast them into a fearful prison, and without admitting the legitimate protestation and defense of their innocence, he cut some of them in two, others he burned at the stake, of others he castrated the men and tore out the breasts of the women. He afflicted them with other divers kinds of torture, until, as it is said, they confessed with their mouth what their conscience did not dictate, choosing to be killed in one moment of agony than to live and be afflicted with torments and tortures."[14]

The Medieval period was an era of almost constant insecurity for Jews. They never knew when a new rumor would surface, accusing them of some act against the community and God. The decision to require all Jews to wear clothing that clearly marked them as Jews, only encouraged the hostility that was present already. Continued ignorance of the Talmud meant the repetition of the old accusation that it was a blasphemous book which led the Jews away from Moses and the prophets. A minimal knowledge of the teaching of the Talmud would have put such charges to rest.

MARTIN LUTHER, "FRIEND" OF THE JEWS

Although the Protestant Reformation brought about widespread change in the religious life of Christian Europe, the lot of the Jews improved but little. At first Martin Luther, the colossus of the Reformation in Germany, was friendly to Jews and appreciative of their traditions. Aware of their inhumane treatment under the Medieval Church, Luther declared:

> For our fools—the popes, bishops, sophists, and monks—the coarse blockheads! have until this time so treated the Jews that to be a good Christian one would have to become a Jew. And if I had been a Jew and had seen such idiots and blockheads ruling and teaching the Christian religion, I would rather have been a sow than a Christian. For they have dealt with the Jews as if they were dogs and not human beings.[15]

THOSE DAMNED JEWS

But, later on, Luther's attitude changed. He became disillusioned when Jews refused to respond to his invitation to convert to Christianity. In anger he turned upon them and repeated the customary charges against them.

> What then shall we Christians do with this damned, rejected race of Jews? . . . Since they live among us and we know about their lying and blasphemy and cursing, we cannot tolerate them if we do not wish to share in their lies, curses, and blasphemy. In this way we cannot quench the inextinguishable fire of divine rage (as the prophets say) nor convert the Jews. We must prayerfully and reverentially practice a *merciful severity.*[16]

Practicing this "merciful severity," Luther advocated that those in power burn Jewish homes and synagogues, destroy

Jewish prayerbooks and the Talmud, forbid rabbis to teach, force Jews to give up their wealth and draft young Jews for hard labor. Finally, Luther urged that Jews be expelled from Germany if "we are afraid that they might harm us." He concludes his tract against the Jews by suggesting to the princes and nobles, to whom he has written, that "if this advice of mine does not suit you, then find a better one so that you and we may all be free of this insufferable devilish burden—the Jews."[17]

SOME DISAGREED

There were, of course, those who were critical of Luther's violent outbursts against the Jews. Not everyone agreed with him! Bullinger, a Swiss theologian, wrote that Luther's anti-Jewish tract sounded like it had been written " 'by a swineherd and not by a renowned shepherd of the soul.' "[18] His words are hardly those of a reformer who has recovered the gospel of Jesus Christ! It is painful to recall these ugly statements of Luther. No wonder they are often passed over quickly by Christians when the story of the Reformation is told.

JEWS WANT TO RULE THE WORLD

Unfortunately, hostility toward the Jews did not cease with Luther. In the post-Reformation years, they continued to be singled out as a sinful and dangerous people. Although there were periods in which Jews enjoyed greater freedom and acceptance (e.g., the Enlightenment), in general, the old attitudes remained alive to threaten the community. Numerous antisemitic tracts made their appearance. They were read, believed, and often written, by Christians. The ready acceptance of these publications guaranteed further harassment and persecution. The depth of suspicion and antagonism toward the Jews may be seen in the popularity of a slanderous tract that originated in Russia as late as 1905. It is titled the *Protocols of the Elders of Zion.* The tract pretends to be a copy of a declaration made by Jews who attended a Zionist Congress in 1897. Jews are made to incriminate themselves as those who conspire to bring about anarchy in the world, so that they may emerge as world leaders.

> "We will establish a central world government of great splendour and complete despotism. The wheels of the machines of every state move on fuel which is in our hands—gold. We will set up a supra-government and subjugate all resisting countries by war, if necessary by a world war. Everywhere in Europe and, through our relations with Europe, in other continents too, we must sow discord, hostility and unrest. After our final victory we will root out all other religions; only the Jewish faith shall be allowed to exist. Should the *goyim* dare to rise against us, we will answer them with the guns of America or China or Japan."[19]

To any informed, fair-minded person, this writing is pure nonsense. But to people raised on the belief that the Jews represented some dark force in the world, it was a believable document. This forgery has spanned the world since its publication. In Germany, especially, it was immensely popular, providing Hitler with a justification for his oppressive measures against the Jews.

THE HOLOCAUST

With Hitler's rise to power Jews entered an era of terror, inconceivable even to the Jewish community itself which, through the years, had endured both persecution and mass slaughter (for example, the murder of vast numbers of Jews in mid-seventeenth century Poland). The Nazi leader's inferno brought incredible suffering to millions of people, but no one people suffered as did the Jews. Following years of state-planned harassment and oppression, a Final Solution to the "Jewish Problem" was found. The solution was death. Jews were killed simply because they were Jews. Six million persons were murdered in gas chambers, fiery ovens, machine gun pits, medical experiments, and in other ways conceived by minds gone strange. Some people today question whether a full six million died. The number is not exaggerated. The documents of the Nazis themselves argue for the credibility of this number. But suppose there were only (!) four million or one million, would the horror be any the less?

THE HOLOCAUST AND THE CHURCH

Among the various factors that contributed to the Nazi Holocaust, Christian hostility to the Jews ranks near the top. In fact, the war against the Jews could never have taken place if it had not been for the anti-Jewish stance of the Christian Church. The Holocaust did not happen all at once. The fires of the furnaces had been heating up for 1900 years. Centuries of misunderstanding and estrangement exploded in a deadly outpouring of hate. Pious Christians, who were able to believe that Jews were shamelessly wicked, came to feel, with Hitler, that they deserved whatever happened to them.

Although a number of Christian leaders in Europe and the United States protested the Nazi oppression, a large part of the Church (also some Jewish leaders!) was indifferent to what was happening. In Germany, Poland, Hungary, and Rumania, many people in the Church actually cooperated with the Nazi program. Hitler had persuaded them that he was only doing what the Christian Church itself had done to the Jews for the last fifteen hundred years.[20] In a number of instances this appears to be true. Raul Hilberg has shown that Hitler's restrictive acts parallel the various decrees, which the early and Medieval Church adopted against the Jews.[21] For example, certain synods and councils prohibited Jews from marrying Christians, eating with them, and employing them as servants. Jews also were deprived of full rights in the courts and were not allowed to receive academic degrees. Further, they were required to wear a badge that clearly identified them as Jews. In other edicts Christians were forbidden to consult Jewish doctors, live in Jewish homes, attend Jewish services, and rent or sell to Jews. All of these ordinances were revived in the laws enforced by the Nazis. Also the Nazi book burnings were preceded by the Church's own fire for the Talmud. Although the Church never condoned the killing of Jews (that was Hitler's contribution), Hitler's basic attitude toward Jews was not alien to the thought of many within the Church.

HEARING THE WHOLE STORY

To blot out the dark actions associated with Christianity is a strong temptation for Christians. The happenings in Germany from 1930 to 1945 do not make pleasant reading for us. We would rather avoid that period of time. Or, if we do talk or write about these years, we prefer to stress the courageous activity of Christians, who risked their lives to help the Jews. There *were* many Christians who did just that. This story must be told. But a mass of evidence points to the existence of large numbers of Christians, who were either apathetic about what was taking place, or who thought that concentration camps were a fitting punishment for the Jews. We must hear the *whole* account, both the good and the bad. That the Church has done much good in the world cannot be denied. Unfortunately, that is not the complete story. Unchristian acts of the past must be confronted and repudiated, if the witness of the Church is to possess integrity.

DISTORTION

How does one explain the existence of hostility to the Jews within the Christian tradition? Why did people, who rejoiced in the unmerited love of God in Jesus Christ, deal so harshly with them? Why were so many restrictions placed upon them? Why did good Christians support the burning of the Talmud and, finally, allow the burning of the people who read the Talmud? Of the many "reasons" for this behavior, misinformation ranks as an important one. Although accurate information about the Jews does not guarantee right action, without it the possibility of repression is great. The various accusations against the Jews would not have been seriously considered if people had been informed about the nature of Jewish faith and life. But where there is lack of knowledge about a people, one begins to believe almost anything about them. Usually one believes the worst instead of the best.

DO JEWS STILL SACRIFICE?

We live in the post-Holocaust era. The grim facts of that terrible event are still fresh to the mind. We have seen how misinformation led to lies and half-truths about the Jews. People were willing to believe the worst. The result was harassment, persecution, and ultimately, the Final Solution. Although, today, there is a greater flow of information between Jews and Christians, the life and literature of Judaism still remains an "unknown" to most Christians. For example, now and then, I have been asked if Jews still offer sacrifice. No, not for the last 1900 years! Misunderstanding concerning the moral character of the ancient Israelites is prevalent also. A recent writer views them as almost complete failures in living out the will of God! Many Sunday School lessons on "Judaism, in the time of Jesus" continue to characterize the religion of that time as a dead, degenerate, sterile faith, one that was empty of joy and fulfillment.[22] There can be little hope of change for the better in Jewish-Christian relationships if such ideas are accepted as truth, for the present day Jewish community is the inheritor of the so-called "sterile" and "empty" first century Judaism.

A STEP TOWARD BETTER RELATIONSHIPS

In a small volume one cannot write about everything! This book is an attempt to provide some basic information about ancient and modern Judaism. I have focused on the ideas of Law and Love, because I believe these important themes in Judaism suffer distortion when Christians begin to talk about them. If one ignores the Jewish witness concerning these teachings, it will be impossible to arrive at a just appraisal of Judaism. Hopefully the following chapters will provide reliable information about Jewish thought and, in this manner, be a contribution to improved Jewish-Christian relationships.

NOTES

1. The above two references are quoted by Rosemary Ruether, *Faith and Fratricide: The Theological Roots of Anti-Semitism* (New York: The Seabury Press, 1974), pp. 127, 130. Used by permission of The Seabury Press. Dr. Ruether's valuable book has been most helpful in the writing of this chapter.
2. Quoted by Malcolm Hay, *Europe and the Jews: The Pressure of Christendom on the People of Israel for 1900 Years* (Boston: Beacon Press, 1960), p. 31.
3. Ruether, p. 146.
4. Hay, p. 26.
5. Quoted by James Parkes, *The Conflict of the Church and Synagogue: A Study in the Origins of Antisemitism* (Philadelphia: The Jewish Publication Society, 1961), p. 101.
6. Quoted by A. Roy Eckardt, *Your People, My People: The Meeting of Jews and Christians* (New York: Quadrangle, 1974), p. 17.
7. Ruether, p. 152.
8. Quoted by Ben Zion Bokser, *Judaism and the Christian Predicament* (New York: Alfred A. Knopf, 1967), pp. 313-314.
9. Frank E. Talmage (ed.), *Disputation and Dialogue: Readings in the Jewish-Christian Encounter* (New York: KTAV, 1975), p. 134.
10. Reuther, p. 153.
11. See Cecil Roth, *Gleanings: Essays in Jewish History and Art* (New York: Herman Press, 1967), pp. 1-19 and Jacob Marcus, *The Jew in the Medieval World* (New York: Atheneum, 1974).

12. Quoted by Solomon Grayzel, *The Church and the Jews in the XIIIth Century* (New York: Herman Press, 1966, revised edition), p. 245.
13. *Ibid.,* pp. 251-253.
14. *Ibid.,* p. 265.
15. Talmage, p. 33.
16. *Ibid.,* pp. 34-36. Emphasis is mine.
17. *Ibid.,* p. 36.
18. Quoted by Friedrich Heer, *God's First Love: Christians and Jews Over Two Thousand Years,* translated by Geoffrey Skelton (New York: Weybright and Talley, 1970), p. 134. Copyright 1967 Bechtle Verlog, Munich and Esslingen. English translation copyright 1970 Weidenfeld and Nicolson, Ltd. Reprinted by permission of the David McKay Company, Inc.
19. *Ibid.,* p. 143. See pp. 141-44 for a discussion of the *Protocols of the Elders of Zion.*
20. See Alan T. Davies, *Anti-Semitism and the Christian Mind: The Crisis of Conscience After Auschwitz* (New York: Herder and Herder, 1969), p. 59.
21. Raul Hilberg, *The Destruction of the European Jews* (New York: New Viewpoints, 1973), pp. 5-6.
22. See the study of Gerald S. Strober, *Portrait of the Elder Brother: Jews and Judaism in Protestant Teaching Materials* (New York: The American Jewish Committee and the National Conference of Christians and Jews, 1972), pp. 16, 21-22.

FOR FURTHER READING

The following books offer the reader a reliable overview of the nature of Jewish-Christian relationships since the first century. Schweitzer's volume is probably the best "first book" for the beginner.

Flannery, Edward H. *The Anguish of the Jews: Twenty-three Centuries of Anti-Semitism.* New York: Macmillan, 1965. Paper.

Hay, Malcolm. *Europe and the Jews: The Pressure of Christendom on the People of Israel for 1900 Years.* Boston: Beacon Press, 1960.

Heer, Friedrich. *God's First Love: Christians and Jews Over Two Thousand Years.* New York: Weybright and Talley, 1970.

Schweitzer, Frederick M. *A History of the Jews Since the First Century A.D.* New York: Macmillan, 1971. Paper.

Chapter Two

OLD TESTAMENT LAW, A DIVINE GIFT

The commandments are a gift of a compassionate God. Mount Sinai may have been clouded in mystery when the Law was given, but an ancient Jewish commentary on the book of Exodus declares that on Sinai God revealed himself as "an old man full of mercy."[1] For many of us the God who spoke at Sinai is quite different. He is a God of strict Law—austere and distant. But is this the God of the Old Testament? Is this the God that Moses and the prophets knew?

SAVED BY GRACE

A central theme of the Old Testament proclaims that Israel owes her existence to the gracious God. He acted on her behalf even when she did not deserve it. God heard the cry of some Hebrew slaves in Egypt. He intervened and delivered them from the mighty power of Pharaoh. He brought them through the burning desert and gave them the land of Canaan. Why did God do that? Not because Israel was the most virtuous member of the human race (Deut. 9:4-6). Certainly not! Even when God was acting to deliver her from Egyptian oppression, she proved unfaithful to him (Ps. 106:6-12). Why then did God continue to lead her? Why did he create a nation out of these rebellious slaves? It was a mystery to Israel. She knew she did not deserve her good fortune. The only explanation that made sense to her was the confession that God rescued Israel because he loved her, and was faithful to the promise given the patriarchs (Deut. 7:8).[2] Her existence as a people was rooted in a God who loved her *before* she ever loved him. Long before Israel gathered at the foot of Mount Sinai, God shared his love with her. The Old Testament writers give witness to what they knew to be the truth: Israel's life as a people was a gift of God.

TORAH IS TEACHING

But what about the Law (*torah*) given at Sinai? What significance did it have for Israel and for her relationship to God? Does *it* reflect God's love for his people? Before answering this specific question, it should be noted that "law" is not an adequate translation for the Hebrew term, *torah*. The word "law" reminds us of strict, legal formulations and of the punishment that comes to those who fail to observe them. It calls to mind the court house with attorneys and judges. It seems to speak of a legalistic relationship between God and his people. There is some truth in the ideas conveyed by the term "law," but a better rendering of *torah* is "instruction" or "teaching." Although the terms "law" or "commandment" will be used interchangeably with the latter terms on the following pages, the preferred translation of *torah* is "teaching."

THE SAVIOR SPEAKS FROM SINAI

What is the nature of this Teaching? How does it relate to God's merciful deliverance of Israel from Egypt? The answer is found in the biblical passages that speak about the giving of the Law. It was no strange God that revealed this Teaching to Israel. The one speaking from Mount Sinai was the gracious God who, with a stunning display of love and power, rescued her from slavery. Introducing the texts which record the various laws, is a clear statement that identifies the Divine Lawgiver as "the LORD your God, who brought you out of the land of

Egypt, out of the house of bondage." (Exod. 20:2) At Sinai, Israel's *Savior* addressed her and said something like this: "You were a slave in Egypt—weak, without strength. Life was oppressive and you were unable to enjoy fully the life given you. I saw your misery, had compassion on you and delivered you from it. You are now a free people. If what I have done means anything at all to you, let it be evident in your relationships to other people. Share with others the same kind of loving concern that I have shared with you."

A RESPONSE TO LOVE

In other words the Law is *not* some legal code that Israel must obey in order to *earn* God's love. Rather it has to do with *Israel's response* to this magnificent love which brought God to the aid of the Israelites in Egypt. What is the character of this response? A look at the various teachings demonstrates that they summon people to a *way of living in the everyday world.* In this respect Sinai is at one with the New Testament. *Both the Old and New Testaments demand a practical response to the love of God.*

REFLECTING CHRIST

Paul frequently emphasizes this point. He declares that one's whole manner of living will reveal how seriously he is related to the love that God has shown in Christ. He points out that bitterness, anger, slander, and malice will not characterize the person who has made a genuine response to this love. Rather the sincere Christian, remembering the forgiveness he has received in Christ, will be kind and tender-hearted to others (Eph. 4:31-32; cp. Gal. 5:16-25). Paul is not talking about becoming more virtuous so that one may earn God's love. He is declaring that when one has experienced the kindness of God, that same kindness will be reflected in one's life.

YOU WERE IN EGYPT AND . . .

The behavior that the Law asks of Israelites is essentially the same as that expected of Christians in the New Testament. At its center the Old Testament radiates a gentle spirit. Its teachings are varied. Some stress honesty and integrity in business dealings. One acts in this manner because this is the kind of God that Israel met in Egypt.

> "You shall do no wrong in judgment, in measures of length or weight or quantity. You shall have just balances, just weight, a just ephah, and a just hin: I am the LORD your God, who brought you out of the land of Egypt."
>
> (Lev. 19:35-36)

Many other teachings express special concern for the poor, the weak, and the disadvantaged. Here also the motivation for showing kindness is the memory of the mercy that God had shown Israel in Egypt. The compassionate God rescued a slave people in the land of Pharaoh and gave them life and hope. These former slaves, remembering the pain of their life in Egypt as well as the joy that came with their release, are called upon to be gentle to others who live difficult lives. The spirit of Old Testament teaching may be discovered in the following passages.

> "If there is among you a poor man, one of your brethren, in any of your towns within your land which the LORD your God gives you, you shall not harden your heart or shut your hand against your poor brother, but you shall open your hand to him, and lend him sufficient for his need, whatever it may be. . . . You shall give to him freely, and your heart shall not be grudging when you give to him; . . . You shall open wide your hand to your brother, to the needy and to the poor, in the land."
>
> (Deut. 15:7-11)

> "You shall not pervert the justice due to the sojourner or to the fatherless, or take a widow's garment in pledge."
>
> (Deut. 24:17)

"When you reap the harvest of your land, you shall not reap your field to its very border, neither shall you gather the gleanings after your harvest . . . you shall leave them for the poor and the sojourner."

(Lev. 19:9-10)

"When a stranger sojourns with you in your land, you shall not do him wrong. The stranger who sojourns with you shall be to you as the native among you, and you shall love him as yourself; for you were strangers in the land of Egypt: I am the LORD your God."

(Lev. 19:33-34)

"You shall not afflict any widow or orphan."

(Exod. 22:22)

"You shall not pervert the justice due to your poor in his suit. Keep far from a false charge, and do not slay the innocent and righteous, for I will not acquit the wicked. And you shall take no bribe, for a bribe blinds the officials, and subverts the cause of those who are in the right.

"You shall not oppress a stranger; you know the heart of a stranger, for you were strangers in the land of Egypt."

(Exod. 23:6-9)

LAWS OF ANOTHER KIND

The above passages represent only a small selection of laws found in the Old Testament. Many others exist which touch various aspects of life, including the family, agriculture, sexual relationships, and worship. Some of these laws are bound to a time long past, as, for example, the laws concerning sacrifice. Sometimes the commandments reflect the harshness of that ancient day:

"A man or a woman who is a medium or a wizard shall be put to death; they shall be stoned with stones, their blood shall be upon them."

(Lev. 20:27)

"Whoever sacrifices to any god, save to the LORD only, shall be utterly destroyed."

(Exod. 22:20)

These laws were rarely enforced by post-biblical Judaism. Over a period of time they were hedged about with so many restrictions that they were in effect set aside. They do not represent the central thrust of Hebrew Law.

THE PROPHETS

What *is* at the heart of Israelite Teaching is clearly seen in the prophets, who are primarily proclaimers and interpreters of the Law. They arose in a time when Israelite society was becoming urbanized and secularized. Respect for the ancient teachings and the old way of life had eroded. The rituals of worship were still observed, but the rights and needs of the weak were ignored. The powerful adopted a spiritualized form of religion that enabled them to "worship" God while living unprincipled lives. There was no lack of sacrifices, but basic morality was forsaken.[3] Irresponsibility too often characterized Israel's rulers, judges, priests, and prophets.[4] The poor and weak—the people without clout— suffered under their care.[5] Forgotten was the God of the Exodus, who gave life to some slaves in Egypt. Rejected was the God of Sinai, who had called Israel to reflect the divine kindness in everyday activities.

THE CENTRAL THRUST

In this period[6] of moral chaos, the prophets called Israel back to the Law with its basic two-fold emphasis: love for God *and* love for persons. They denounced those who thoughtlessly "performed" the religious rituals of prayer, sacrifice, and offering. The rituals themselves were not condemned, but ritual observance, that had little relationship to the way one lived, earned their wrath. In the thought of the prophets, true worship goes beyond rituals and manifests itself in compassion for peo-

ple. Micah's impressive words express what was central to the
law and to the great prophets of Israel:

> He has showed you, O man, what is good;
> and what does the LORD require of you
> but to do justice, and to love kindness,
> and to walk humbly with your God?
>
> (Mic. 6:8[7])

That love for God and love for persons comprise the basic
elements of Old Testament Teaching, may be seen from an
ancient summary of the Law which is at the core of Jewish
faith. It is also quoted with approval by Jesus himself (Luke
10:25-28).

> You shall love the LORD your God with all your heart, and with
> all your soul, and with all your might.
>
> (Deut. 6:5)
>
> Love your neighbor as yourself.
>
> (Lev. 19:18)
>
> This emphasis lies at the root of Judaism as well as Christianity.
> In both communities any profession of love for God becomes a
> mockery, if it is not accompanied by genuine concern for other
> human beings.

THE LAW IS LIFE

The Teaching of the Old Testament calls for a life response
to the love of God. It declares that one does not genuinely love
God, unless there is kindness and fairness in relationship to
others. No doubt corrupt rulers, dishonest judges, and the in-
sensitive rich considered this teaching to be a burden. It
cramped their style! They wanted to be free from the Law so
that selfish goals could be pursued unhindered. But to the poor
and disadvantaged, the Law was no burden. It was life. Here
was evidence of God's concern for them.

IT IS JOY

However, the Law was not only protection for the unfortunate. It nourished all who set their hearts upon it, including the influential as well as the average person. Obedience to this divine Teaching brought about a full and satisfying life. It was a gift which one received with rejoicing and thanksgiving. The Law is life-giving like the sun, declares Psalm 19. The first part of this psalm speaks of the grandeur of the sun as it moves through the heavens (vss. 1-6). Verses 7-10 are a hymn extolling the greatness of the Law.

1 The heavens are telling the glory of God;
   and the firmament proclaims his handiwork.
2 Day to day pours forth speech,
   and night to night declares knowledge.
3 There is no speech, nor are there words;
   their voice is not heard;
4 yet their voice goes out through all the earth,
   and their words to the end of the world.

In them he has set a tent for the sun,
5 which comes forth like a bridegroom leaving his chamber
   and like a strong man runs its course with joy.
6 Its rising is from the end of the heavens,
   and its circuit to the end of them;
   and there is nothing hid from its heat.

7 The law of the LORD is perfect,
   reviving the soul;
the testimony of the LORD is sure,
   making wise the simple;
8 the precepts of the LORD are right,
   rejoicing the heart;
the commandment of the LORD is pure,
   enlightening the eyes;
9 the fear of the LORD is clean,
   enduring for ever;
the ordinances of the LORD are true,
   and righteous altogether.

10 More to be desired are they than gold,
    even much fine gold;
sweeter also than honey
    and drippings of the honeycomb.

Both the heavens and the Law reveal the glory of God! The psalmist stands in awe of the sun and its majestic movement through the heavens. But he recalls also the Law which, like the sun, brings life, joy, and light to the world. It appears that the author is comparing the Law to the Sun. Several terms that are used to describe the Law were also employed in the ancient world to speak of the sun, for example, the words "pure" and "enlightening" in verse 8. In any case the psalm as a whole testifies to the joy of the worshiper as he thinks of the Law. It is to be desired more "than gold, even much fine gold." It is "sweeter also than honey and drippings of the honeycomb." (Vs. 10) The delight that the Law created in the hearts of pious Israelites also finds witness in many other psalm passages (e.g., Pss. 1 and 119).

THE LAW IS FOREVER

A Teaching that produces such happiness should never be set aside! The Old Testament views the Law as eternally valid. It will never come to an end. When the prophets speak about the time when God's kingdom will come fully into being, they describe it in terms of the teachings of Sinai. In such an age, justice and righteousness will prevail and the poor will receive due consideration.[8] A future that did not include the Law would be a future without the compassion of God.

THE NEW TESTAMENT

The joy with which Israel embraced the Law sometimes causes surprise to Christians, because the Church is familiar with another view of the Law. It is represented in the writings of the Apostle Paul who sometimes speaks of the Law in negative terms. It is something dark, accusing, and inadequate: "the law brings wrath."[9] However, at this point it should be noted that there is another view of the Law in the New Testament. In the books of Luke and Acts, one finds appreciation for this ancient Teaching.[10] There is no indication that the Law is a burden, or that it was no longer valid following the coming of Christ.

JUDAISM

At its center, Rabbinic Judaism continued the positive view of Law found in the Old Testament. It was thought to be the bread of life for Israel. Without it Israel would perish. However, one should not overlook the fact that there were legalistic persons in the Old Testament period as well as in post-biblical Judaism. These people created burdens for themselves and others. But such people are not confined to any one religion. Through the centuries, representatives of this kind of thinking and living have had their influence in the Christian Church. But they do not represent the fundamental stance of Christianity. The same is true with regard to Israelite faith.

NOTES

1. Lauterbach, vol. 2, p. 31 (Shirata, Exod. 15:5-6). See Chapter Six Notes for complete bibliographical information.
2. This promise ("oath") mentioned in Deuteronomy 7:8 is also rooted in God's love. Abraham did nothing to earn this promise even though he responded in obedience when God called him. The election of Abraham and the promise given him, originate in the mystery of divine grace.
3. Hosea 4:1-2; Jeremiah 7:8-10
4. Micah 3:9-12
5. Amos 2:7; 5:10-11; 7:4-6
6. Although the prophet was an ancient figure in Israel (e.g., Moses, Samuel, and Nathan), the great prophetic movement began with Elijah and Elisha (ca. 850 B.C.). Amos, Hosea, and Isaiah followed about a century later. Under the monarchy Israel began to cultivate contacts with surrounding

countries. Trade developed, a merchant class came into being and cities began to grow. People left the farm country and moved to the cities. The old tribal way of living (which emphasized responsibility for others) was forgotten. Without the restraint of a close community, and led on by a desire for wealth and power, many indulged their selfish desires. Among such people the weak could only expect oppression. In this time of disorder, the prophets were the voice of God calling Israelites to return to the teaching given them at Sinai. It is a mistake to think that the prophets were men who brought some new teaching to Israel. A reading of their oracles reveals that their basic message was the Teaching of Sinai.

7. See also Isaiah 1:16-17; 58:6-9; Jeremiah 7:5-7; 22:15-16; Amos 5:21-24 etc.
8. Isaiah 9:7; 11:1-5; Jeremiah 23:5-6
9. Romans 4:15. Cp. Romans 3:20; 5:20; 6:14; Galatians 3:2 f. etc.
10. Luke 10:25-37; Acts 21:17-26

FOR FURTHER READING

Childs, Brevard S. *The Book of Exodus.* Philadelphia: Westminster, 1974. A first-rank commentary which views the texts of Exodus in the context of the New Testament as well as that of the Old Testament. Although it is somewhat technical, certain sections will provide important information for the layperson (e.g., "The Decalogue and the New Testament," pp. 428-31).

Heschel, Abraham J. *The Prophets, I-II.* New York: Harper & Row, 1969. Paper. A fascinating study of the prophets of Israel by a renowned Jewish scholar. Chapter One entitled "What Manner of Man Is the Prophet?" is an excellent description of the message of the prophet and its relationship to Old Testament Law.

Hubbard, David A. *Psalms for All Seasons.* Grand Rapids: Eerdmans, 1971. Paper. Chapter One is a brief meditation on Psalm 1.

Hummel, Horace D. "Law and Grace in Judaism and Lutheranism," in *Speaking of God Today: Jews and Lutherans in Conversation* (eds., Paul Opsah and Marc Tanenbaum). Philadelphia: Fortress Press, 1974, pp. 15-20. A well informed discussion, which makes some good observations concerning the character of Law in the Old Testament, Judaism, and Paul. See below also the contribution of Michael Wyschogrod in the same volume.

Knight, G. A. F. *Law and Grace.* London: SCM Press, 1962. A useful study of the character of Law in both testaments; written with the layperson in mind.

Muilenburg, James. *The Way of Israel.* New York: Harper & Row, 1961, pp. 31-97. A perceptive study of the Law and the Prophets.

Myers, J.M. *Grace and Torah.* Philadelphia: Fortress Press, 1975. Paper. A superb, brief investigation (86 pp.) of Law and grace in the Old and New Testaments. The lay reader may have difficulty with some of the scholarly discussion and terminology.

Napier, B. Davie. *The Layman's Bible Commentary: Exodus,* Vol. 3. Richmond: John Knox, 1963. A reliable, non-technical commentary. See especially his comments on Exodus 20—23.

Rothschild, Fritz A. (ed.). *Between God and Man: An Interpretation of Judaism.* New York: The Free Press, 1965. Paper. The above book contains selections from the writings of Abraham Heschel. Chapters 26 and 27 relate to the concept of Law in Judaism.

von Rad, Gerhard. *Moses* (World Christian Books). London: Lutterworth Press, 1960. Paper. In Chapter Four: "God's Will as Made Manifest in Law," this influential German scholar presents a brief, readable discussion of what lies at the center of Israelite Law.

Wyschogrod, Michael. "The Law: Jews and Gentiles" in *Speaking of God Today: Jews and Lutherans in Conversation* (eds., Paul Opsah and Marc Tanenbaum). Philadelphia: Fortress Press, 1974. A Jewish scholar looks at Paul's view of the Law against the background of the Old Testament and the teachings of Judaism.

Chapter Three

THE RIGHTEOUS MERCY OF GOD IN THE OLD TESTAMENT

No one is absolutely perfect! It should not surprise us that Israel often disobeyed the Teaching given them by God. Even the most faithful persons in Israel must have broken the Law at one time or another.

FORGIVENESS IS FREE

What happened when Israelites broke the Law? Was forgiveness possible? If so, what was required of the one who sought forgiveness? Yes, forgiveness was possible. But it could not be earned or purchased. How, then? It was given free "without money and without price!" *One needed only to approach God with a sincere heart and ask his forgiveness!* So simple and direct? We have had the impression that forgiveness of sins in the Old Testament is complicated and, in the end, something less than satisfying. But numerous passages in the Psalms testify of a God who freely forgives those who genuinely repent. Psalm 51 comes immediately to mind. The confident mood of the prayer grows out of the psalmist's belief that God responds favorably to persons who seek his forgiveness.

> 1 Have mercy on me, O God,
>   according to thy steadfast love;
> according to thy abundant mercy
>   blot out my transgressions.

2 Wash me thoroughly from my iniquity,
  and cleanse me from my sin!

3 For I know my transgressions,
  and my sin is ever before me.

4 Against thee, thee only, have I sinned,
  and done that which is evil in thy sight,
so that thou art justified in thy sentence
  and blameless in thy judgment.

5 Behold, I was brought forth in iniquity,
  and in sin did my mother conceive me.

6 Behold, thou desirest truth in the inward being;
  therefore teach me wisdom in my secret heart.

7 Purge me with hyssop, and I shall be clean;
  wash me, and I shall be whiter than snow.

8 Fill me with joy and gladness;
  let the bones which thou hast broken rejoice.

9 Hide thy face from my sins,
  and blot out all my iniquities.

10 Create in me a clean heart, O God,
  and put a new and right spirit within me.

11 Cast me not away from thy presence,
  and take not thy holy Spirit from me.

12 Restore to me the joy of thy salvation,
  and uphold me with a willing spirit.

13 Then I will teach transgressors thy ways,
  and sinners will return to thee.

14 Deliver me from bloodguiltiness, O God,
  thou God of my salvation,
  and my tongue will sing aloud of thy deliverance.

15 O Lord, open thou my lips,
  and my mouth shall show forth thy praise.

16 For thou hast no delight in sacrifice;
  were I to give a burnt offering,
    thou wouldst not be pleased.

17 The sacrifice acceptable to God is a broken spirit;
  a broken and contrite heart, O God,
    thou wilt not despise.

GOD LOOKS AT THE HEART

The worshiper in the above Psalm knows that he has done wrong. He has experienced waywardness and perverseness at the center of his life. Although his offenses are serious, causing God great displeasure, he appeals directly to God for forgiveness. His life can only be healed by God himself (vss. 6-12). He does not mention his virtues nor does he attempt to secure favor with God through sacrifice. He is well-acquainted with this ritual, but he knows that repeated sacrifice will not bring about forgiveness. God does not want sacrifice (vss. 15-16). Far more important to him is the quality of a person's heart. When one is repentant there, then God listens and forgives. This, the psalmist understands, for he declares: "The sacrifice acceptable to God is a broken spirit; a broken and contrite heart, O God, thou wilt not despise." (Vs. 17) The sinner who is truly sorry for sins always finds a gracious God.

A WIDENESS IN GOD'S MERCY

Psalm 51 represents the normal way by which one secures forgiveness in the Israelite tradition.[1] From the beginning, Israel knew a gracious God. He delivered Israel from Egyptian slavery when the nation had done nothing to deserve this kind of intervention. In fact, God took action on Israel's behalf while the people were still sinful (Ps. 106:6-12)! The *merciful* God was no stranger to Israel. Many passages in the Old Testament celebrate the compassionate God who welcomes repentant sinners.

> "Seek the LORD while he may be found,
>   call upon him while he is near;
> let the wicked forsake his way,
>   and the unrighteous man his thoughts;
> let him return to the LORD, that he may have mercy on him,
>   and to our God, for he will abundantly pardon."
>
> (Isa. 55:6-7)

The LORD is merciful and gracious,
    slow to anger and abounding in steadfast love.
He will not always chide,
    nor will he keep his anger for ever.
He does not deal with us according to our sins,
    nor requite us according to our iniquities.
For as the heavens are high above the earth,
    so great is his steadfast love toward those who fear him;
as far as the east is from the west,
    so far does he remove our transgressions from us.
(Ps. 103:8-12)

I acknowledged my sin to thee,
    and I did not hide my iniquity;
I said, "I will confess my transgressions to the LORD";
    then thou didst forgive the guilt of my sin
(Ps. 32:5)

If thou, O LORD, shouldst mark iniquities,
    LORD, who could stand?
But there is forgiveness with thee,
    that thou mayest be feared.
(Ps. 130:3-4)

To thee shall all flesh come
    on account of sins.
When our transgressions prevail over us,
    thou dost forgive them.
(Ps. 65:2-3)

The witness of the Old Testament is firm: God's love flows to those in need. His delight is not in punishment; he glories in forgiveness.

THE RIGHTEOUS GOD

However, God's forgiveness does not root only in, what we call, his mercy. He also forgives the sinner because he is the righteous God. Because he is the *righteous* God? In our day we tend to separate righteousness from mercy. Therefore, when someone declares that the God of the Old Testament is a righteous God, the image that comes to mind is that of a stern deity who is morally perfect. Or, we think in terms of a God who is wrathful toward those who do not measure up to his laws.

It is true that the Old Testament writers believe that God is perfect, fully right in all of his ways (Deut. 32:4). But this is not what is usually meant, when he is called the righteous God. Most often, in the Old Testament, God's "righteousness" refers to his dependability and his saving acts. In Hebrew thought there is no basic conflict between the righteous and the merciful God. For this reason the prophet is able to declare that he is "a righteous God and a Savior." (Isa. 45:21) When God is merciful to those in distress, he also reveals himself to be righteous.[2] Similarly people who are compassionate to their neighbors are considered to be righteous.

> He has distributed freely, he has given to the poor;
> > his righteousness endures for ever;
> > his horn is exalted in honor.
>
> > > > (Ps. 112:9)

> Thus says the LORD: Do justice and righteousness, and deliver from the hand of the oppressor him who has been robbed. And do no wrong or violence to the alien, the fatherless, and the widow, nor shed innocent blood in this place.
>
> > > > (Jer. 22:3)

A RIGHTEOUS, SAVING GOD

The Hebrew term, sedaqah, is frequently translated by the word "righteousness." The translation is correct, but it is important to bear in mind that this Hebrew term includes within itself the sense of salvation, vindication, victory, deliverance, and mercy. Sometimes these latter terms are used to translate sedaqah.[3] When the psalmists speak of the righteous God, they do so with joy because such a God brings help and salvation. In the passages which follow, the He-

brew term *sedaqah* will be inserted after the English words
that translate it. These verses are selected to show the saving character of God's righteousness. Notice, that in some
passages, reference to the righteousness of God occurs in
parallelism with a phrase mentioning his salvation or good-
ness.

> My mouth will tell of thy righteous [*sedaqah*] acts,
>   of thy deeds of salvation all the day,
>   for their number is past my knowledge.
> With the mighty deeds of the Lord GOD I will come,
>   I will praise thy righteousness [*sedaqah*], thine alone.
>
>   (Ps. 71:15-16)

> ". . . my deliverance [*sedaqah*] will be for ever,
>   and my salvation to all generations."
>
>   (Isa. 51:8)

> Men shall proclaim the might of thy terrible acts,
>   and I will declare thy greatness.
> They shall pour forth the fame of thy abundant goodness,
>   and shall sing aloud of thy righteousness [*sedaqah*].
>
>   (Ps. 145:6-7)

A person in deep need may direct a plea to the righteous God,
for the God of righteousness is also full of mercy.

> In thee, O LORD, do I take refuge;
>   let me never be put to shame!
> In thy righteousness [*sedaqah*] deliver me and rescue me;
>   incline thy ear to me, and save me!
>
>   (Ps. 71:1-2)

When the Lord intervenes and saves a person from his distress,
he is praised for his rightousness, that is, for his saving help.

> My lips will shout for joy,
>   when I sing praises to thee;
>   my soul also, which thou has rescued.
> And my tongue will talk of thy righteous help [*sedaqah*]
>   all the day long,

for they have been put to shame and disgraced
   who sought to do me hurt.

                                          (Ps. 71:23-24)

THE SINNER AND THE RIGHTEOUS GOD

Even when sin has been committed, a person may appeal to
the righteousness of God, as does Daniel in the following passage.

> . . . we have sinned, we have done wickedly. O Lord, according
> to all thy righteous acts [sedaqah], let thy anger and thy wrath
> turn away from thy city Jerusalem, thy holy hill; because for our
> sins, and for the iniquities of our fathers, Jerusalem and thy people
> have become a byword among all who are round about us.

                                          (Dan. 9:15-16)[4]

Psalm 51:14 also demonstrates that a repentant sinner is
able to rejoice in the righteousness of God. As we noted at the
beginning of this chapter, the psalmist is fully aware of the
seriousness of his sin. He knows that the sin he has committed
is primarily against God. He admits that God will be right in
whatever sentence he chooses to pronounce upon him (vss. 3-4).
Nevertheless, he asks God to have mercy upon him (vss. 1-2)
and, from the remainder of the psalm, it appears that he expects
God to do so. He renews his plea to God in verse 14:

> Deliver me from bloodguiltiness O God,
>   thou God of my salvation,
>   and my tongue will sing aloud of thy deliverance [sedaqah].

God's righteousness (sedaqah) calls forth praise and thanksgiving because it has the character of compassion.

OVERFLOWING LOVE

The God of the Old Testament is mighty in power,
highly exalted and perfect in all his ways. But, as great as is
his power so is his mercy. He is tender to those in need. He

responds with compassion to the sinner who seeks forgiveness. He is righteous, but his righteousness is not cold and repelling. It has the warmth of mercy and the attractiveness of forgiveness. It comes in overflowing measure to all who seek him in sincerity.

NOTES

1. Among other passages, which illustrate the free access the Israelites had to God concerning sin and forgiveness, are the following: Psalms 25:18; 38:18; 39:8; 41:4; 85:2.
2. See Psalm 116:5-6 and Jeremiah 9:24.
3. See, e.g., the following passages: Isaiah 62:1 (vindication); Psalm 65:5 (deliverance); Judges 5:11 (triumph); Psalm 48:10 (victory). When the Hebrew Scripture was translated into Greek (the Septuagint), the Hebrew term *sedaqah* was often rendered by *eleēmosunē* (kindness, mercy).
4. In the verses that follow, Daniel continues the prayer and declares that his request for forgiveness rests on God's *mercy* (vs. 18). In verse 15 Daniel had called upon the righteousness of God. Whether one looks for help from the righteousness or the mercy of God makes little difference.

FOR FURTHER READING

Berkovits, Eliezer. *Man and God: Studies in Biblical Theology.* Detroit: Wayne State University Press, 1969. A lengthy study (57 pp.) in Chapter Seven gives basic information concerning the meaning of righteousness in the Old Testament. Although the use of various Hebrew terms may cause the general reader some hesitation, it is a well written and rewarding discussion.

Gleason, Robert W. *Yahweh: The God of the Old Testament.* Englewood Cliffs, New Jersey: Prentice-Hall, 1964. Relevant material may be found in the chapters entitled: "God Is Just" and "The Love of God."

Heschel, Abraham J. *The Prophets, I-II.* New York: Harper & Row, 1962. Paper. Chapter 11 in Volume I sums up, in a fine manner, the meaning of justice and righteousness in the Prophets.

Hubbard, David A. *Psalms for All Seasons.* Grand Rapids: Eerdmans, 1971. Chapter 13 presents a meditation of Psalm 51.

Klassen, William. *The Forgiving Community.* Philadelphia: Westminster,

1966. Contains three excellent, readable chapters (pp. 19-100) on for-giveness in the Old Testament, Pre-Christian Judaism, and the New Testament. A bibliography is included.

Kuitert, Harry M. *Signals from the Bible.* Grand Rapids: Eerdmans, 1972. Paper. Clear, non-technical discussion of righteousness and re-demption in biblical literature. See especially Chapters 11, 12, and 19.

Myers, J.M. *Grace and Torah.* Philadelphia: Fortress Press, 1975. The last chapter of this important study, "Salvation and Torah in the New Testament," focuses on the book of Romans. In attempting to under-stand the message of this book, the author also gives attention to the themes of salvation, grace, and love occurring in the Old Testament.

Weiser, Artur. *The Psalms.* Philadelphia: Westminster, 1962. A helpful commentary which achieves a good balance between devotion and scholarship. See especially the author's interpretation of Psalm 51.

Chapter Four

SACRIFICE, A SYMBOL OF INNER COMMITMENT

"It's a bloody book," said a friend to me after I had told her of my plans to become a seminary professor. "Why do you want to teach the Old Testament?" She had in mind the sacrificial system described in the Hebrew Bible. No doubt many people have similar thoughts about the Old Testament. The idea of sacrifice is repugnant to us, but people of an ancient time valued it as a sacred act. Why was sacrifice offered? What meaning did it have?

A LONG TIME AGO

Long before the existence of Israel, sacrifice was a firmly established custom in the Near East. Although sacrifice in Israel had a special character, the practice of sacrifice itself was an act that Israel shared with other ancient peoples, for example, the Canaanites and the Babylonians.

In an age when herdsmen and farmers represented the main occupations of people, it is understandable that worship of God would be expressed through an act in which an animal or some agricultural product would be *given* to him. The "sacrifice" of grain does not offend our sensibilities, but animal sacrifices are alien to our thought. Their bloody and seemingly cruel character repels us. However, for the herdsman of a long ago day, animal sacrifice was a natural act. He slaughtered animals to provide food for his family, so it did not seem out of the ordinary to have an animal "slaughtered" for God.

WORSHIP GOD WITH SACRIFICES

In the Old Testament, sacrifice appears as an act of worship which incorporated various meanings. Sometimes the worshiper simply wished to express love for God by giving him the sacrifice on the altar. Also sacrifice was a way of seeking God's blessing upon one's work as a herdsman or farmer. For example, the farmer gave to God a portion of the *first* harvest of the crops and the herdsman sacrificed the *first*born of the herd. By these actions they were confessing: "Without you, O God, there is no harvest; apart from you there is no increase of the herd. We acknowledge your life-giving power in this world by offering you the firstfruits of the harvest and the firstborn of the herd. Accept them and *continue* to bless our efforts as farmers and herdsmen."

Sometimes a meal was eaten in connection with a sacrificial offering (e.g., the Peace offering). The worshiper would invite his relatives and friends to come to the sanctuary so that they might share a meal from what was offered to God upon the altar (cp. Deut. 12:7, 18; 14:23). God and those who loved him shared in the same sacrifice! The meal celebrated the peace and friendship that existed between them.

IF YOU DID NOT MEAN TO . . .

But sacrifice had another purpose. This ritual was to be performed when one *unintentionally* disobeyed the will of God and, in so doing, broke the peaceful union existing between God and oneself. In such a situation special sacrifices served as a means by which one's sin was removed. By offering these sacrifices one re-established the harmonious relationship with God.

What is the character of the sacrifice for sin? In Leviticus 4, several similar rituals are described. The one for the ordinary person is set forth in Leviticus 4:27-31.

"If any one of the common people sins unwittingly [i.e., unintentionally] in doing any one of the things which the LORD has commanded not to be done, and is guilty, when the sin which he has committed is made known to him he shall bring for his offering a goat, a female without blemish, for his sin which he has committed. And he shall lay his hand on the head of the sin offering, and kill the sin offering in the place of burnt offering. And the priest shall take some of its blood with his finger and put it on the horns of the altar of burnt offering, and pour out the rest of its blood at the base of the altar. And all its fat he shall remove, as the fat is removed from the peace offerings, and the priest shall burn it upon the altar for a pleasing odor to the LORD; and the priest shall make atonement for him, and he shall be forgiven."

NOT AUTOMATIC

Unwittingly, without premeditation, a person has transgressed the will of God. When this sin is called to his attention, he responds with a repentant heart. He did not *intend* to sin. It was done in ignorance. But this error has interrupted the relationship with God, therefore something must be done to re-establish this bond of friendship. The sacrificial ritual described above provides a way back. But the ritual does not operate automatically. It assumes sincere sorrow on the part of the person who offers the sacrifice.

REMEMBERING THE POOR

It is difficult for us, at this late date, to understand fully the meaning or meanings contained in the sacrifice for sin. In reading the descriptions of the various rituals, we must be careful lest we make too much of certain words, sentences, or actions performed. When we speak about a "sin offering" we tend to think of an animal, the laying on of hands, the death

of the animal, and blood on the altar. But was it absolutely
necessary for a sin offering to take this form? No! If a person
was too poor to make the animal sacrifice, an alternative offering was acceptable. Such a person could bring to the priest
some flour and

> "the priest shall take a handful of it as its memorial portion and
> burn this on the altar, upon the offering by fire to the LORD; it
> is a sin offering. Thus the priest shall make atonement for him
> for the sin which he has committed in any one of these things,
> and he shall be forgiven. And the remainder shall be for the
> priest, as in the cereal offering."
>
> (Lev. 5:12-13)

BLOODSHED NOT NECESSARY

From the above text, it is clear that blood need not be shed
in order to bring about removal of sin. In a very simple ritual,
one may offer flour; it is accepted as a sin offering! The book
of Hebrews declares (9:22, my emphasis): "Indeed, under the
law *almost* everything is purified with blood, and without the
shedding of blood there is no forgiveness of sins." Blood sacrifice *is* very prominent in the Old Testament, but an alternative
is permissible. The word *almost* is very important in the above
quote from Hebrews, and it should be seen as a qualification of
the whole sentence. The sin offering did not *demand* a blood
sacrifice. A grain offering was acceptable.

A SYMBOLIC ACTION

The sacrifice that God wants is "a broken and contrite
heart." (Ps. 51:17) This was not a new thought introduced by
the author of the psalm. It was a basic element of Israelite faith.
Sacrifice was a symbolic action. It was assumed that when one
offered a sacrifice for the unintentional sin he had committed,
the outward sacrifice reflected a heart that was truly sorry for
the wrong that was done. It was this attitude of sorrow that
gave validity to the sacrifice on the altar.

RITUALS POINT BEYOND THEMSELVES

Everything good is capable of being abused and perverted. Rituals are good. Rituals are bad. They are good when they point to something deeper in the relationship between God and the person. Rituals are bad when they become automatic, and the essentials of faith are forgotten. Every religious community knows the problem of keeping rituals "alive." In the Christian tradition the Lord's Supper and baptism are rich in meaning, yet all too frequently people participate in a mechanical manner.

THE PROPHETS SPEAK

Sharp words were spoken on the subject of religious cere-mony by the prophets. One basic thought underlay their words in this area. All ritual, they said, must reflect genuineness of heart if it is to be accepted by God. The Israelite sacrificial system fell under fierce prophetic denunciation because, in the mind of the prophets, it violated this primal principle. It was a right attitude of heart, symbolized in the sacrificial act, that pleased God. The prophets speak with passion at this point. Sacrifices offered by insincere persons mock God and make him angry. The words of Amos are representative of the prophetic censure.

"I hate, I despise your feasts
  and I take no delight in your solemn assemblies.
Even though you offer me your burnt offerings and cereal offerings,
  I will not accept them,
and the peace offerings of your fatted beasts
  I will not look upon.
Take away from me the noise of your songs;
  to the melody of your harps I will not listen."
                              (Amos 5:21-23)

God hates these feasts and sacrifices, because they do not reflect a people intent on doing the will of God in this world. The sacrifices do not come from the heart. If the sacrifices were from sincere hearts, then there would be justice and righteousness in the community. People would seek not only their own good but the good of others. Such was not the case in the days of Amos. However, it is this kind of response that God really wants: " 'But let justice roll down like waters, and righteousness like an ever-flowing stream.' " (Amos 5:24) The eloquent words of Micah convey the same message (Mic. 6:6-8):

> "With what shall I come before the LORD,
>   and bow myself before God on high?
> Shall I come before him with burnt offerings,
>   with calves a year old?
> Will the LORD be pleased with thousands of rams,
>   with ten thousands of rivers of oil?
> Shall I give my first-born for my transgression,
>   the fruit of my body for the sin of my soul?"
> He has showed you, O man, what is good;
>   and what does the LORD require of you
> but to do justice, and to love kindness
>   and to walk humbly with your God?

RELIGION WITHOUT SACRIFICE

Abolishment of sacrifice was not the goal of the prophets. Rather, they wanted sacrifice to be what it was meant to be, namely, an act that symbolized the true desire of the heart. But the implication of prophetic preaching is unmistakable; Israelite faith did *not depend* on sacrifice. It was *not necessary* to the continuance of Israel's religion. If circumstances so required, Hebrew faith could get along without sacrifice.

Israel *could* get along without sacrifice. Israel *did* continue her life and faith without it. After the destruction of the Jerusalem temple in 587 B.C., sacrifice became an impossibility for most Jews. Some apparently still offered sacrifice at the ruined temple, but the many Jews who fled, or were deported, to other countries had to find another mode of worship. During this period without sacrifice the faith did not die. Israel prayed to God, felt his judgment but also experienced his love and forgiveness. Some seventy years later, after the Jews were allowed to return to the land, a new temple was built (516 B.C.) and sacrifice was reinstituted.

In 70 A.D., destruction fell upon the temple once again. It would never be rebuilt. Sacrifice came to an end, but the gracious God continued on with his people. For nineteen hundred years the Jewish community has worshiped without sacrifice.

SUPPOSE YOU MEANT TO SIN

One other matter needs attention. The above discussion centered mostly on sacrifice offered because of sin. For sins done *unintentionally* one could offer sacrifice and, if sincere, forgiveness was granted. But what happened in the case of one who sinned with a "high hand," that is, who committed an intentional, premeditated sinful act? What kind of sacrifice was to be offered in such a case? None! According to the following text from Numbers 15:27-31, sacrifices were to be offered for those who committed unintentional sins but none were to be presented on behalf of those who were guilty of premeditated evil acts. They had made firm decisions to commit sin, so they were to be punished.

> "If one person sins unwittingly [i.e., unintentionally], he shall offer a female goat a year old for a sin offering. And the priest shall make atonement before the LORD for the person who commits an error, when he sins unwittingly, to make atonement for him; and he shall be forgiven. You shall have one law for him who does anything unwittingly, for him who is native among the people of Israel, and for the stranger who sojourns among them. *But the person who does anything with a high hand, whether he is native or a sojourner, reviles the LORD, and that person shall be cut off from among his people. Because he has despised the word of the LORD, . . . and has broken his commandment, that person shall be utterly cut off; his iniquity shall be upon him.*" (Emphasis mine.)

FORGIVENESS FOR HIGH-HANDED SINNERS

No specific crime is mentioned in the above text, but presumably murder and adultery would be classified as intentional, high-handed acts. No sacrifices were prescribed for these sins. The Law decreed a death sentence for such acts (Num. 35:16ff.; Lev. 20:10). Was all hope gone then for those who were guilty of these sins? No, forgiveness was still possible. If these high-handed sinners were genuinely sorry for their sins, God granted them forgiveness. Such was the situation of David in his affair with Bathsheba (2 Sam. 11—12). With deliberation he committed adultery and brought about the death of Uriah. He should have been executed but was not. Throwing himself upon the God of grace, the king confessed his sin and his life was spared (2 Sam. 12:13).[2]

IF WITH ALL YOUR HEART

The superscription to Psalm 51 ascribes this psalm to David, in the time "when Nathan the prophet came to him, after he had gone in to Bathsheba." The psalm itself does not reveal the specific nature of the sin, but it is evident that it was consciously committed. Sacrifice would not help. There is no sacrifice for this sin. But there is forgiveness for the sinner—yes, even for the high-handed sinner—whose heart is broken by what he has done and who expresses genuine repentance.

Let me summarize the relationship of sacrifice to sinful acts. Sacrifice may be offered for sins done unintentionally. However, in this situation, sacrifice is not automatically effective. The sacrifice must be offered by a sincere person who deeply regrets the sin committed. Sacrifice was important, but more important was the character of the person who offered the sacrifice. If the person was devious, the sacrifice was of no value. The significance of the person's attitude is seen in the case of one who commits an intentional sin. Sacrificial ritual was not able to handle this kind of a matter. The one who committed such an act stood under divine judgment. But forgiveness was possible, *if* he repented with all his heart.

THE GRACIOUS GOD

While sacrifice was a very important aspect of Old Testament and Jewish faith, it was not an absolute necessity. Israel could, Israel did get along very well without sacrifice. This could happen because, in Hebrew-Jewish religion, God is the gracious God who desires to do good to persons who seek him with a true heart.

NOTES

1. There are a few passages which appear to look upon sacrifice as a way of appeasing the wrath of God (e.g., 2 Sam. 24:25 and Job 1:5). However, this emphasis is not central to the Old Testament view of sacrifice.
2. In 2 Samuel 12:14 the death of David's child is considered to be a punishment for his sin. See a similar case with regard to Ahab (1 Kings 21:29). The subject is a difficult area of discussion because different views are represented in the Old Testament. For example, observe that both Deuteronomy 24:16 and Ezekiel 18 decisively reject the idea that children suffer for the sins of the fathers (cp. Jer. 31:29-30).

FOR FURTHER READING

Dan, Joseph. "Sacrifice," in *Encyclopaedia Judaica* (ed., Cecil Roth). Jerusalem: Keter Publishing House Ltd., 1971. Pp. 599-616.

Gaster, T. H. "Sacrifices and Offerings," in *The Interpreter's Dictionary of the Bible,* Vol. 4 (ed., George Buttrick). New York: Abingdon, 1962. Pp. 147-159.

Ringgren, Helmer. *Sacrifice in the Bible.* New York: Association Press, 1962. Written for the layperson, this book covers the whole area of sacrifice and its meaning in the Old and New Testaments. Excellent.

Rowley, H. H. "The Meaning of Sacrifice in the Old Testament," in *From Moses to Qumran: Studies in the Old Testament* (ed., H. H. Rowley). New

York: Association Press, 1963. Pp. 67-110. Balanced, concise discussion of this difficult area.

Thompson, R. J. "Sacrifice and Offering," in *The New Bible Dictionary* (ed., J. D. Douglas). Grand Rapids: Eerdmans, 1962. Pp. 1113-1122.

de Vaux, Roland. *Ancient Israel: Its Life and Institutions* (trans., John McHugh). New York: McGraw-Hill, 1961. A magnificent work in which a lengthy section is given over to the discussion of sacrifice (pp. 415-456).

de Vaux, Roland. *Studies in Old Testament Sacrifice.* Cardiff: University of Wales, 1964. Matches the excellence of other contributions by this great French scholar. Although some technical and foreign words are used, the orderly and straightforward manner of writing makes this a usuable volume for the layperson.

Chapter Five

THE EARLY LITERATURE OF JUDAISM

A FOREIGN LAND

The Christian enters the world of Jewish literature as an alien. A knowledge of both the Old and New Testaments does not adequately prepare one for a meeting with the enormous literature produced by the rabbis. Words such as Mishnah, Gemarah, Talmud, Midrash, among others, are confusing. How do they relate to each other? What importance do they have for Judaism?

JUDAISM IS . . .

We tend to see Judaism as the religion of the Old Testament. But to do so, is to misunderstand the character of Jewish faith. While Jews revere the ancient Scriptures, Judaism is not to be identified with its Teachings. Rather, Judaism is the religion that has resulted from rabbinic *interpretation* and *expansion* of the Old Testament. Any real appreciation of this faith must begin with an understanding of the writings of the ancient rabbis, preserved in the Mishnah, Talmud, and Midrash.

MISHNAH

The Mishnah is a large body of literature, containing teachings which were handed down by word of mouth over a long period of time. The word mishnah means "repetition." Thus, the term indicates the original oral character of the material. That is, for many years these teachings were preserved by means of one generation *repeating* them to the next generation. The Mishnah is sometimes called the "Oral Law" because it was, *at one time,* passed on by word of mouth. Now, however, these teachings are in written form. Tradition has it that they were copied down about 200 A.D. It is difficult to determine how far back in time these teachings go. No doubt some of them derive from the first century A.D.—or even earlier.

THE MISHNAH INTERPRETS THE SCRIPTURES

The material in the Mishnah represents an "authoritative" interpretation of the laws found in the Pentateuch. Sometimes, the Old Testament Law is lacking in detailed information on how one should observe what was commanded. For example, references concerning marriage and divorce occur in the Law, but there is no full information given about *arrangements* for marriage or *procedure* in the case of divorce. The Mishnah spells out what is to be done on these occasions. In other cases, mishnaic instruction softened some of the harsh teachings of the Old Testament, by surrounding them with so many qualifications that they could not be enforced. In general, the teaching of the Mishnah attempted to fit the Old Testament Law to new times and new situations. However, it also preserved traditions that had little contemporary relevance. By the time the Mishnah was formulated, the temple had been in ruins for over a hundred years. Nevertheless, a rather large part of this literature is given over to temple architecture, various sacrifices, and rituals. The transmission of teaching in these areas gives the Mishnah an archaic character.

In certain teachings the Mishnah comments on matters that

receive no mention at all in the Old Testament Law. For example, a whole tractate is given over to instruction on the observance of the New Year festival (Rosh Hashanah). Nevertheless, for the most part, the Mishnah represents an interpretation of the commandments recorded in the Pentateuch. These laws were considered to be God's will for the community, therefore the rabbis thought it of first importance to find out what, *specifically,* one should do to obey God.

THE MISHNAH NEEDS INTERPRETATION

Even though the Mishnah is a bulky literature (about 800 pages in English), it could not cover every question that might arise concerning the observance of the Law. Time moved on. Succeeding generations brought new rabbis, new situations, and new questions. The Mishnah, which had interpreted and expanded the teaching of Scripture in the light of a new day, now needed itself to be interpreted and expanded! Later rabbis subjected the Old Testament Law and the Mishnah to searching inquiry, and commented on the teaching recorded in the Mishnah. These comments constitute the Gemarah. This latter term has the meaning of "completion" and indicates that the comments of these rabbis give a more complete explanation of what is found in the Mishnah.

THE TALMUD

The Mishnah and Gemarah together form the Talmud (teaching). It is a multi-volumed literature (34 volumes in English), which assumed its present form about 500 A.D. The Talmud quotes the text of the Mishnah along with the comments of various rabbis (Gemarah). In their remarks, the rabbis attempt to blend common sense with the Scriptural Law.

THE TALMUD DEALS WITH SPECIFICS

The rabbis were "lawyers," and the mind of the lawyer is easily observable in the talmudic discussions. For this reason, it has come to be known as a "legalistic" literature. However, before judgments are formed, several comments are in order. The rabbis were concerned about doing God's will in, what we would call, the secular world. Therefore, they gave instruction in civil and criminal law (for example, regarding property damage, personal injury, theft, murder). Awareness of the complicated nature of our own civil and criminal codes today, will make us less critical of the efforts of the rabbis in this area.

Further, the rabbis were responsible for guidance in the religious sphere of life. People looked to them for an answer to the question: how should a Jew live before God? Because this question was usually asked with regard to a *specific issue,* it demanded a *specific reply.* Many questions plagued the rabbis! What should one do on the Sabbath? How should various holy days be celebrated? When death occurs, what should be done? What should one do when a serious disease is contracted? What is the "right" thing to do when one marries? When one is divorced? What is the proper relationship between men and women? Still, today, rabbis attempt to give guidance concerning these and other questions.

THE TALMUD AND THE CHURCH

Within the Christian tradition, there is nothing fully comparable to the varied and detailed discussions of the Talmud. However, the writings of the Church Fathers, and the decisions of various Church councils, reveal similar concerns. Christian leaders, as well as Jewish rabbis, were forced to confront specific problems and make specific judgments as to what constituted the will of God. For example, to mention only a few, the early Church handled such issues as: the nature of Christian worship, the observance of Easter, fasting and prayer, visiting preachers, apostates, the celebration of the Eucharist, and the practice of baptism. In recent years the Church has made pronouncements on such specific issues as: contraception, ordination of women, liturgy, relationships with other Christian and non-Christian groups, service in the armed forces, and abortion. These discussions concerning the right response to specific issues, which every devout person faces, may have a higher visibility in Judaism, but they are not missing in the life of the Church. A religion that seeks to be helpful in the everyday experiences of its followers, must address specific issues.

MIDRASH: IMAGINATIVE COMMENTARY

Midrash exists as a form of commentary on the books of the Old Testament. The word midrash roots in a Hebrew term which means "to examine or seek." Midrash does not deal with the surface meaning of a biblical text. It is not interested in explaining the factual or literal meaning of a Scripture passage. Rather, a rabbi, who prepares a midrashic commentary on a biblical book, attempts to "get underneath" the text and seek out its hidden meaning. Midrash is imaginative interpretation of the text. It often has a homiletical and devotional character, and uses stories, legends, and parables in making its point. Someone has said that Midrash should never be viewed literally, but must always be taken seriously. Although the commentary itself may be fanciful, the theology expressed often reflects the basic affirmations of Judaism. Some of these commentaries date from about 200 A.D. and possibly earlier.

FOR FURTHER READING

Adler, Morris. *The World of the Talmud.* Second edition. New York: Schocken, 1963. Paper. Brief, readable discussion of talmudic literature and thought.

Cohen, Abraham. *Everyman's Talmud.* New York: Dutton, 1949. Citations from the Talmud together with the author's comments. Helpful.

Corre, Allan, (ed.). *Understanding the Talmud.* New York: KTAV, 1975. Paper. Essays by top scholars on a wide variety of subjects relating to the Talmud, its background, and religious ideas. Some of the articles may prove "tough" to handle, but the studious layperson will find excellent material here.

Lipman, Eugene, (ed.). *The Mishnah: Oral Teachings of Judaism.* New York: Norton and Company, 1970. Following an introduction entitled "What Is Mishnah?" the author summarizes important sections of the Mishnah. Written for the general public.

Montefiore, C. G. and H. Loewe. *A Rabbinic Anthology.* New York: Schocken, 1974. Scholars agree that this magnificent volume is the best anthology of the mishnaic, talmudic, midrashic literature. "A delight to read, a treasure to own."

Neusner, Jacob. *Invitation to the Talmud.* New York: Harper and Row, 1973. An excellent guide into the *character* of rabbinic thought. Especially important for the reader are the first and last chapters, entitled respectively, "The Talmud in Context" and "Talmudic Thinking and Us."

Neusner, Jacob, (ed.). *Understanding Rabbinic Judaism: From Talmudic to Modern Times.* New York: KTAV, 1974. Paper. The title says it all. A twenty page bibliography.

Chapter Six

JEWISH TEACHING ON THE LAW

THE LAW (TORAH) IS THE WILL OF GOD

Judaism is the religion of Torah. While generally, the term "Torah" applies to the teaching of the Pentateuch, it may also refer to the whole of the Hebrew Scripture. But Torah, however conceived, was seen to be God's revelation of his will for Jews. Every phrase of Scripture, and each word of the phrase, was considered to be from God himself. The words of the Torah were the words that God selected to be there. One must study them carefully, for in "cracking open" these words one finds a treasure—the will of God for the living of this life. In the words of the Law, there is instruction for all times and situations. Thus, it is said of the Torah in the Mishnah: "Turn it and turn it over again, for everything is therein, and contemplate it, and wax gray and old over it, and stir not therefrom, for thou canst have no better principle than this."[1] God will not hide his will from the one who seeks it in earnest study.

STUDY AND OBEY

The purpose of the study of the Law was the practice of it in everyday life. Obedience was the point of it all. Study that did not lead finally to conduct, was considered useless before God.

And thus Moses, when he had the privilege of receiving the Torah, first recited a blessing, and then he read it. R. Eleazar asked: What was the blessing which Moses recited before reading it? It was, Blessed art Thou, O Lord, King of the Universe, who hast chosen this law and sanctified it and hast found pleasure in them who fulfil it. He did not say, "in them that labour at it," nor, "in them who meditate in it," but, "in them that fulfil it," that is to say, in them who carry out the words of the Torah.[2]

Although the rabbis placed great stress on *doing* the Law, they never seem to have thought that if persons disobeyed one or more laws they were then under the fierce, irreversible judgment of God. Absolute perfection was not demanded of people. It was recognized that God was not pleased when one sinned, but the rabbis believed in a God who granted forgiveness to those who repented and sincerely attempted to do his will.

REWARDS

The rabbis taught that good things happened to those who obeyed the Torah. Sometimes they talk about the great rewards that come to those who study and practice the Law. While there may have been people who were "reward-conscious," there are many warnings in the rabbinic literature against obedience for the sake of reward. The Law was to be studied and practiced for its own sake.

Antigonus of Socho received the tradition from Simon the Just. He used to say, Be not like servants that minister to the master on the condition of receiving a reward, but be like servants that minister to the master without the condition of receiving a reward; and let the fear of heaven be upon you.[3]

BEYOND LEGALISM

The legal character of rabbinic writings (especially the Talmud) is immediately apparent to the reader. But, as we have noted previously,[4] it would be unfair to identify this literature as surface, legalistic material. That the rabbis were sometimes unduly exacting, in specifying what should and should not be done, is not denied. However, it is clear also that these leaders were able to see *the* Law, which formed the basis for the many laws they expected people to obey. Specific commandments were needed to give guidance on specific issues that arose from day to day, and from generation to generation. But these many commandments simply reflected a *basic teaching* handed down by God to his people. The following legend about two great Jewish teachers (roughly contemporary with Jesus) illustrates this awareness of what was fundamental.

> On another occasion it happened that a certain heathen came before Shammai and said to him, "Make me a proselyte, on condition that you teach me the whole Torah while I stand on one foot." Thereupon he repulsed him with the builder's cubit which was in his hand. When he went before Hillel, he said to him, "What is hateful to you, do not to your neighbour: that is the whole Torah, while the rest is commentary thereof; go and learn it."[5]

613 COMMANDMENTS EQUALS ONE

Beautifully illustrating the ability of the rabbis to see *basic Law* under the many commandments, is the following passage in the Talmud, which is attributed to a rabbi of the third Christian century. He declares that six hundred and thirteen laws were given to Moses on Mount Sinai. This teaching is often viewed as evidence that the Jews carried a heavy burden of Law. Six hundred and thirteen commandments to obey! Suppose one keeps 612 of them but breaks the 613th one? Too bad?! To approach the passage in this manner is to miss the point completely. The rabbi is declaring, that the many laws given the Jews, are only extensions of a few basic commandments which God has written deep in the heart of humankind.

R. Simlai when preaching said: Six hundred and thirteen precepts were communicated to Moses. . . . David came and reduced them to eleven [Ps. 15] . . . Isaiah came and reduced them to six principles [Isa. 33:15], . . . Micah came and reduced them to three principles, as it is written, *It hath been told thee, O man, what is good, and what the Lord doth require of thee: (1) only to do justly, and (2) to love mercy and (3) to walk humbly before thy God.* . . . Again came Isaiah and reduced them to two principles, as it is said, *Thus said the Lord, (1) Keep ye justice and (2) do righteousness.* . . . Amos came and reduced them to one principle, as it is said, *For thus said the Lord unto the house of Israel, Seek ye Me and live.* To this R. Nahman b. Isaac demurred saying: Might it not be taken as, Seek Me by observing the whole Torah and live? —But it is Habakkuk who came and based them all on one principle, as it is said, *But the righteous shall live by his faith.* [6]

TORAH GIVES STRENGTH

When one studies and obeys the Law he not only receives insight as to how he should live, but he also *obtains strength* to live that kind of life. Within each individual, say the rabbis, there is a Good Inclination and an Evil Inclination.[7] The Evil Inclination, if left unchecked, would lead us to ruin. But obedience to the Law strengthens the Good Inclination and gives the individual power to resist and overcome the Inclination to evil. God helps those who seek to do his will!

"*Thy word have I laid up in my heart, that I might not sin against Thee* (Ps. 119:11). The Inclination-to-evil has no power in the presence of the Torah. And so the Inclination-to-evil has no power over him who has Torah in his heart, and cannot touch him.[8] Blessed is Israel; when they occupy themselves with Torah and acts of kindness, their [evil] inclination is mastered by them, not they by their [evil] inclination.[9]

THE TORAH IS NO BURDEN

The Law is God's gift of love to his people. It is something good for Israel. The idea that the Torah was some dark cloud hanging over one's head is foreign to rabbinic thought. It was light, not darkness. It was eagle's wings, not a heavy rock. It was kindness and gentleness, not wrath.

> "Why does it say, 'A heap of wheat set about with lilies (Cant. VII, 2)? This refers to Torah. Have you ever heard of a man who made a fence of lilies? People hedge their fields and vineyards with thorns or brambles. But the words of Torah are soft and gentle.[10]

The study and practice of Torah brings health and a full life. It is often compared to those things that nourish the body or create pleasure for a person, namely: water, oil, honey, wine, and milk.

> Just as water makes plants grow, so the words of the Torah nurture everyone who labours over them as they require. . . . *And wine that maketh glad the heart of man* (Ps. 104:15), so words of Torah rejoice the heart, as it says, *The precepts of the Lord are right, rejoicing the heart* (Ps. 19:9). . . . just as oil makes the head and the body feel pleasant, so the words of the Torah make the head and body feel pleasant, as it says, *Thy word is a lamp unto my feet* (Ps. 119:105). . . . it is compared to milk and honey: just as these are sweet throughout, so are the words of the Torah, as it says, *Sweeter also than honey* (Ps. 19:11).[11]

The one who lives this life without Torah, is depriving himself of divine food and drink! While the above comments on the character of Torah are marked by "poetic exaggeration," a reading of rabbinic literature makes clear that the Law did not cast a dark shadow in the Jewish community. Those who ignored its teachings, and remained unrepentant, came under divine judgment. But the purpose of Law was not to bring punishment. A gift of a gracious God, it pointed to life, not death.

TORAH AND LIFE TO COME

God, who has given the Torah to humanity, is also the one who has created this life and the life to come. The Law sustains and enriches life in the here and now world. But it also opens the door to the life to come.

> He that has gained a good name has acquired a gain for himself; one who has acquired for himself words of the Law has gained for himself life in the world to come.[12]

> In the hour of man's departure, neither silver nor gold nor precious jewels nor pearls accompany him, but only the reputation of knowledge of the Law and good works, as it is said, *When thou walkest it shall lead thee, when thou liest down it shall watch over thee; and when thou awakest it shall talk with thee;* 'when thou walkest it shall lead thee'—in this world; 'when thou liest down it shall watch over thee'—in the grave; 'and when thou awakest it shall talk with thee'—in the Hereafter.[13]

No sad songs were sung in Israel when God gave the Torah to Moses. It was a day that called for celebration. On it God revealed his "way" to Israel. It was a way of life in the everyday world, and it led to fullness of life in the world to come.

NOTES

Citations from rabbinical writings are taken from the following volumes unless otherwise noted.

THE MISHNAH
> Philip Blackman (ed.), *Mishnayoth.* Seven volumes. New York: The Judaica Press, 1963-65.

THE TALMUD
> Isidore Epstein (ed.), *The Babylonian Talmud.* Thirty-four volumes. London: The Soncino Press, 1935-48.

MIDRASH
> H. Freedman and M. Simon (eds.), *Midrash Rabbah.* Ten volumes. London: The Soncino Press, 1939. Used with permission.

> Jacob Z. Lauterbach (ed.), *Mekilta de-Rabbi Ishmael.* Three volumes. Philadelphia: Jewish Publication Society of America, 1933-35. Copyrighted by and used through the courtesy of The Jewish Publication Society of America.

> William G. Braude (ed.), *The Midrash on Psalms.* Two volumes. New Haven: Yale University Press, 1959. Used with permission.

1. Blackman, Avoth 5:22, p. 538 (Order Nezikin).
2. Freedman and Simon, vol. 7, p. 177 (Deut. 11:6).
3. Blackman, Avoth 1:3, p. 490 (Order Nezikin).
4. See Chapter Five.
5. Epstein, Shabbath 31a, p. 140 (Seder Mo'ed).
6. Epstein, Makkoth 23b-24a, pp. 169-73 (Seder Nezikin). The quotation does not represent a continuous text.
7. The rabbis approach life as practical people. In attempting to understand the presence of good and evil within humankind, they *describe* what happens within us. There is little interest in a philosophical explanation of good and evil. They see within every person a desire for the good and a desire for the evil. This is the human situation! The practical bent of rabbinic thought is further seen in the observation that the inclination to evil is not completely evil. In fact, strange as it may sound to Christian ears, it is said that God created the inclination to evil and pronounced it good!

   Nahman said in R. Samuel's name: BEHOLD, IT WAS VERY GOOD refers to the Good Desire; AND BEHOLD, IT WAS VERY GOOD, to the Evil Desire. Can then the Evil Desire be very good? That would be extraordinary! But for the Evil Desire, however, no man would build a house, take a wife and beget children; and thus said Solomon: *Again, I considered all labour and all excelling in work, that it is a man's rivalry with his neighbour* (Eccl. IV, 4).

   The inclination to evil pushes us to "look out" for ourselves. But this inclination is dangerous. It tends to lead persons beyond wholesome concern for oneself to ruinous behavior. For this reason it must come under the control of Torah. The above passage is cited from the Midrash Rabbah (Genesis) 9:7, in the Freedman and Simon edition, p. 68. For a lengthy discussion of the Evil Inclination, see Solomon Schechter, *Aspects of Rabbinic Theology* (New York: Schocken, 1961), pp. 242-292.
8. Braude, vol. 2, p. 256 (Psalm 119:11).
9. Epstein, 'Abodah Zarah 5b, p. 22 (Seder Nezikin).
10. Quoted by C. G. Montefiore and H. Loewe, *A Rabbinic Anthology* (New York: Schocken, 1974), p. 156. (Pesikta Rabbati 35b)
11. Freedman and Simon, vol. 9, pp. 33-35 (Song of Songs 1:2). The quotation does not represent a continuous text.
12. Blackman, Avoth 2:7, p. 500 (Order Nezikin).
13. Blackman, Avoth 6:9, p. 549 (Order Nezikin).

FOR FURTHER READING

Cohen, Abraham. *Everyman's Talmud.* New York: Dutton, 1949. See Chapter 4 on "Revelation."

Corre, Allan, (ed.). *Understanding the Talmud.* Paper. New York: KTAV, 1975. See the following articles: G. F. Moore, "The Idea of Torah in Judaism"; Louis Finkelstein, "Life and Law"; and Julius Guttman, "The Religious Ideas of Talmudic Judaism."

Heschel, Abraham. *God in Search of Man.* Paper. New York: Harper and Row, 1966. Section Three, which concerns one's response to God's revelation of himself, gives insight into the rabbinic view of Law.

Moore, George F. *Judaism in the First Centuries of the Christian Era,* I. Cambridge, Mass.: Harvard University Press, 1927. See Chapters Three and Four, entitled respectively, "The Unwritten Law" and "Perpetuity of the Law."

Montefiore, C. G. and H. Loewe. *A Rabbinic Anthology.* Paper. New York: Schocken, 1974. A rich mine of material on the Law is found in Chapters Five through Eight.

Neusner, Jacob, (ed.). *The Life of Torah: Readings in the Jewish Religious Experience.* Encino, California: Dickenson, 1974. Paper. Nine brief chapters are given over to the concept of Torah in Judaism. The book is a fine source for information about Jewish religious thought.

Parkes, James. *Prelude to Dialogue: Jewish-Christian Relationships.* New York: Schocken, 1969. Chapter Three: "The Meaning of Torah."

Schechter, Solomon. *Aspects of Rabbinic Theology.* New York: Schocken, 1961. Four chapters (8-11) are given to the topic of Law in rabbinic Judaism.

Chapter Seven

JEWISH TEACHING
ON THE LOVE OF GOD

FIVE HUNDRED YEARS AWAY

Do you know where God is? Yes! To reach God you must travel a distance of five hundred years, then five hundred more and five hundred more and more and more and more, so says the Talmud.[1] What is being said? It is the rabbinic way of declaring that God stands immeasurably beyond this universe and everything finite. He is highly exalted above all that we know and see.

FAR AWAY BUT NEAR

Because there are many passages in rabbinic literature which stress the transcendent character of God, it is sometimes thought that the God of the rabbis is far removed from people and their needs. Christian writers have often referred to such passages to show that Judaism does not know the warmth of God's closeness. But rabbinic thought often exhibits a "both/and," rather than an "either/or" theology. For the rabbis, God is *both* transcendent over *and* yet fully near to us. Though far "beyond" the world which he has created, he observes all that happens, and hears the faintest cry for help. To those in need he is immediately available. No mediator is needed to reach him.

And God is distant and yet near. How? R. Judah b. Simon said: From here [the earth] unto heaven is a journey of five hundred years; hence He is distant. Whence do we know that He is also near? A man stands at prayer and meditates in his heart and God is near unto his prayer.[2]

If a man is in distress, let him not call on Michael or Gabriel, but let him call direct on me, and I will hearken to him straightway.[3]

OUR FATHER

Not too many years ago, it was commonly believed that the concept of God as father was almost unknown in Judaism. However, a glance at Jewish literature reveals that God's fatherhood is a central theme in rabbinic thought. God is often given the title of "father," and the imagery of divine fatherhood occurs repeatedly in the writings of the rabbis.

Ye shall not afflict any widow, or fatherless child (Ex. 22:21). R. Jose said: Why does God love orphans and widows? Because their eyes are raised to none but Him, as it says, *A father of the fatherless, and a judge of the widows* (Ps. 68:6); hence he who robs them is like one who robs God, their Father in heaven. . . .[4]

And the Angel of God . . . Removed, etc. R. Judah says: This is a verse rich in content, being echoed in many places. To give a parable, to what is this like? To a man who is walking on the road with his son walking in front of him. If robbers who might seek to capture the son come from in front, he takes him from before himself and puts him behind himself. If a wolf comes from behind, he takes his son from behind and puts him in front. If robbers come from in front and wolves from behind he takes the son up in his arms. When the son begins to suffer from the sun, his father spreads his cloak over him. When he is hungry he feeds him, when he is thirsty he gives him to drink. So did the Holy One, blessed be He, do, as it is said: "And I, I taught Ephraim to walk, taking them upon My arms; but they knew not that I healed them" (Hos. 11.3). When the son began to suffer from the sun, He spread His cloak over him, as it is said: "He spread a cloud for a screen," etc. (Ps. 105.39). . . .[5]

"Our Father, Our King," are the initial words of a prayer commonly attributed to Rabbi Akiba, a celebrated teacher who lived in the second century of our era. This beautiful, and confident, appeal for God's grace and help, is recited still today in Jewish worship. It speaks of the God who is far off (king of the universe) but yet near (father). In alluding to the closeness and distance of God, it reminds one of the opening line of the Lord's Prayer: *"Our Father* who art *in Heaven."*

> Our Father, Our King, be gracious to us and answer us, for there is little merit in us. Treat us generously and with kindness, and be our help.[6]

MAGNIFICENT IN LOVE

God transcends this world and all that is human, not only because he is the creator but also because he is the compassionate one. The generosity of his love for people is quite other than the limited concern persons share with each other. This love is a constant presence with those that seek to obey him. But, it is also a love that surrounds the one who rebels against his Law. This does not mean that God is lax concerning evil doing. Numerous passages in rabbinic literature stress his judgment of the one who sins. Nevertheless, although he is strict in upholding his commandments, his heart has full love for the sinner. He does not glory in inflicting pain. When he must punish, it is with a heavy heart, even though the judgment is deserved. In the punishment, God himself suffers. He says: " 'My head is in pain, My arm is heavy'."[7]

JUSTICE AND MERCY

If God took note of every sin, no person would remain standing before him. Fortunately, he is not that kind of God! With the psalmist (Ps. 130), the rabbis rejoice in One who is both just and merciful. God never acts according to "pure" justice, that is, justice apart from mercy. A striking passage in

the Talmud, portrays God "praying" that his mercy will overcome both his anger and justice.

> Hence you learn that the Holy One, blessed be He, says prayers.
> What does He pray?—R. Zutra b. Tobi said in the name of Rab:
> "May it be My will that My mercy may suppress My anger, and
> that My mercy may prevail over My other attributes, so that I may
> deal with My children in the attribute of mercy and, on their
> behalf, stop short of the limit of strict justice."[8]

The following passage also speaks of his compassionate relationship with a sinful world.

> Yet Rab Judah said in the name of Rab: "The day consists of
> twelve hours; during the first three hours the Holy One, blessed
> be He, is occupying Himself with the Torah, during the second
> three He sits in judgment on the whole world, and when He sees
> that the world is so guilty as to deserve destruction, He transfers
> Himself from the seat of Justice to the seat of Mercy."[9]

I AM SORRY

God delights in mercy. He is constantly hopeful that he can
save rather than destroy. With tender heart he seeks reconciliation with those who have rebelled against him. He is willing—
always—to forgive. Whether he does or not, rests with the
person. The heart that meets God with repentance is quickly
and fully embraced by divine love.

> . . . the Holy One, blessed be He, said:I—My hands reach out to
> the penitent. I turn back no man who gives me his heart in repent-
> ance.[10]

> "A king had a son who had gone astray from his father a journey
> of a hundred days; his friends said to him, 'Return to your father';
> he said, 'I cannot.' This his father sent to say, 'Return as far as
> *you* can, and *I* will come to you the rest of the way.' So God says,
> 'Return to me, and I will return to you.' "[11]

> "If your sins are as high as heaven, even unto the seventh heaven,
> and even to the throne of glory, and you repent, I will receive
> you."[12]

The following passage depicts a father's forgiveness of a wayward son who wants to return home, but is ashamed to do so.

THOU WILT RETURN TO THE LORD THY GOD [Deut. 4:30]. R. Samuel Pargrita said in the name of R. Meir: This can be compared to the son of a king who took to evil ways. The king sent a tutor to him who appealed to him saying, "Repent, my son." The son, however, sent him back to his father with the message, "How can I have the effrontery to return? I am ashamed to come before you." Thereupon his father sent back word, "My son, is a son ever ashamed to return to his father? And is it not to your father that you will be returning?" Similarly, the Holy One, blessed be He, . . .[13]

PREPARE THE WAY FOR HUMANKIND

The importance attached to repentance may be seen in the following passage. Before God created the universe, he brought into existence seven things, one of them being repentance.

Surely it was taught: Seven things were created before the world was created, and these are they: The Torah, repentance, the Garden of Eden, Gehenna, the Throne of Glory, the Temple, and the name of the Messiah.[14]

Naturally, the Torah stands first in the above list because it represents God's revelation of himself. However, repentance is listed next. The idea seems to be, that before creation, God knew that people would not be able to do his will perfectly. Therefore, he formed "repentance" so that humankind would have a "way back" into full fellowship with him!

NO MERIT IN DEPENDING ON OTHERS

Sometimes people call attention to the rabbinic teaching concerning the "merits of the fathers" to which, it is believed, Jews look to cover or balance their sinful acts. The teaching is more complicated than it appears to be. It would be wrong to think that this teaching refers to a treasury of merits, which a

Jew could use to achieve favor with God. While Israel might benefit from the existence of pious ancestors, the "merits of the fathers"[15] do not take the place of repentance. Rather it seems to express the kind of corporate thinking so characteristic of Israel. One is always related to the past and to the future. The existence of the fathers, and the promises made to them, give Israel the "right" to call upon God. But the deeds of pious ancestors are unable to save a rebellious person who decides to remain rebellious. Only repentance—an honest turning around —brings about reconciliation between God and humanity. Of the many passages that could be quoted, the following one is to the point.

> A man has no right to put his trust in the works of his forebears. Ishmael has no right to say: "Abraham is my father, I am a part of him, and he will help me." Esau has no right to say: "Jacob was righteous, and he will help me; by virtue of his works I shall be redeemed." For the verse *No man can by any means redeem his brother* (Ps. 49:8) means that a man's brother cannot redeem him; if a man does no good in this world, he has no right to put his trust in the works of his forebears.[16]

THE GOOD NEWS

As is well-known, the election of Israel is a very prominent theme in both the Hebrew Scripture and the rabbinic literature. Numerous passages in the latter material express joy about the special relationship that Israel has with God. Therefore, when the rabbis speak about the relationship between God and humanity, most often they are thinking of God's relationship to Israel and to Jews. All of the passages we have quoted above have their primary reference in the Jewish community. There are other passages that mention the Gentiles, both positively and negatively, but a discussion of these references is not the purpose of this chapter. The concern of these pages has been to highlight some aspects of God's relationship to his people. Too frequently rabbinic Judaism is represented as a cold faith, which does not know the kind and generous God. The passages quoted above, reveal that the rabbis shared the good news of a loving God with the Jewish community. The God whom they knew was a Father who suffered in the sufferings of his children, one who longed for the companionship of those he had created.

NOTES

Citations from rabbinical writings are taken from the following volumes unless otherwise noted.

THE MISHNAH
> Philip Blackman (ed.), *Mishnayoth.* Seven volumes. New York: The Judaica Press, 1963-65.

THE TALMUD
> Isidore Epstein (ed.), *The Babylonian Talmud.* Thirty-four volumes. London: The Soncino Press, 1935-48.

MIDRASH
> William G. Braude (ed.), *The Midrash on Psalms.* Two volumes. New Haven: Yale University Press, 1959.

> H. Freedman and M. Simon (eds.), *Midrash Rabbah.* Ten volumes. London: The Soncino Press, 1939.

> Jacob Z. Lauterbach (ed.), *Mekilta de-Rabbi Ishmael.* Three volumes. Philadelphia: Jewish Publication Society, 1933.

1. Epstein, Hagigah 13a, p. 74 (Seder Mo'ed).
2. Freedman and Simon, vol. 7, pp. 38-39 (Deut. 2:10).
3. C. G. Montefiore and H. Loewe, p. 23. (Palestinian Talmud)
4. Freedman and Simon, vol. 3, p. 354 (Exod. 30:8).
5. Lauterbach, vol. 1, pp. 224-25 (Beshallah, Exod. 14:16-21).
6. See *Gates of Prayer: The New Union Prayerbook,* published by the Central Conference of American Rabbis, p. 392.
7. Blackman, Sanhedrin 6:5, p. 264 (Order Nezikin).
8. Epstein, Berakoth 7a, p. 30 (Seder Zera'im).
9. Epstein, 'Abodah Zarah 3b, p. 9 (Seder Nezikin).
10. Braude, vol. 2, p. 293 (Psalm 120:7).
11. C. G. Montefiore and H. Loewe, p. 321. (Pesikta Rabbati 184b-185a)
12. *Ibid.,* p. 320. (Pesikta Rabbati 185a)

13. Freedman and Simon, vol. 7, p. 53 (Deut. 2:24).
14. Epstein, Pesahim 54a, p. 265 (Seder Mo'ed).
15. See Solomon Schechter, *Aspects of Rabbinic Theology* (New York: Schocken, 1961), pp. 170-198, for an understanding of this concept in Jewish thought.
16. Braude, vol. 2, pp. 363-64 (Psalm 146:2).

FOR FURTHER READING

Cohen, Abraham. *Everyman's Talmud.* New York: Dutton, 1949. See pp. 16-22 (Justice, Mercy, and Fatherhood of God) and pp. 104-110 (Repentance and Atonement).

Montefiore, C. G. and H. Loewe. *A Rabbinic Anthology.* New York: Schocken, 1974. Extensive citations from rabbinic literature on God's love and repentance are found in the following chapters: 1-4, 8, 12.

Moore, George F. *Judaism in the First Centuries of the Christian Era.* Cambridge, Mass.: Harvard University Press, 1927. Chapters 5-7 in Volume I provide a lenghty discussion (40 pages) on Repentance and Forgiveness.

Schechter, Solomon. *Aspects of Rabbinic Theology.* New York: Schocken, 1961. Chapters 17 and 18 address themselves to the topics of Forgiveness and Repentance.

Chapter Eight

THE PHARISEES
AND JESUS

THE DIFFICULTY OF BEING IMPARTIAL

A balanced view of the Pharisees is difficult to achieve. A long standing representation of them in the Jewish and Christian communities makes it almost impossible to consider them without prejudice. Further complicating the problem is the meager amount of information we possess, that can be dated with certainty, from the time of the Pharisees. The eyewitness literature is limited to the first century writings of the New Testament and Josephus.[1] The portrayal of them in the Gospels is largely negative while that found in Josephus is usually a favorable one. Neither of these sources present a fully objective picture of the Pharisees. The view of Josephus is probably influenced by his own commitment to the Pharisaic way of life. He speaks from the "inside" and therefore is generally sympathetic to the movement. On the other hand, the followers of Jesus are involved in conflict with the Pharisees. The Gospel writers reflect the controversy that Jesus and the early Church had with them. Little wonder then that the Pharisees frequently appear in an unfavorable light.

THE TRADITION OF VERBAL OVERKILL

The fierce condemnation of the Pharisees in Matthew 23 is well-known. They are represented as: hypocrites, blind guides, blind fools, whitewashed tombs, serpents, brood of vipers, and people who preach but do not practice. Various attempts have been made to understand the character of this passage. Some scholars compare it to the denunciations of the ancient prophets, who used harsh terminology in their censure of the Israelite nation. Thus, in the first chapter of Isaiah, Israel is called Sodom and Gomorrah, a "sinful nation, a people laden with iniquity." (1:4) Israel's rulers are "rebels and companions of thieves" (1:23) and, the prophet declares, "Every one loves a bribe." (1:23) The indictment of Israel by Micah 3:9-11 is equally uncompromising:

> Hear this, you heads of the house of Jacob,
>   and rulers of the house of Israel,
> who abhor justice
>   and pervert all equity,
> who build Zion with blood
>   and Jerusalem with wrong.
> Its heads give judgment for a bribe,
>   its priests teach for hire,
>   its prophets divine for money.

The above judgments are severe. They must be taken seriously, but not literally. The texts seem to say that the whole nation is sinful, that all of Israel's rulers are corrupt, that there is no justice in the land, that everyone is false and unreliable. But, if anyone perceived these passages in this manner, it would surely represent a gross misunderstanding of Israelite faith in the time of the prophets. It is generally understood that the prophets speak in exaggerated language, as do most present-day preachers, when they attack the evils of society. What appears to be an indictment of every citizen in Israel, of every priest and prophet, is in actual fact an arraignment of some, or perhaps many, of these persons.

THE DEAD SEA SCROLLS

In attempting to understand Matthew 23, attention has been called also to the literature of the Qumran community. Here one finds violent language used of the "opposition." Following are some selections from one of the hymns preserved by the community.

> But as for *them*—
> they have [dealt treacherously] with Thee,
> have made smooth their words.
> Garblers of truth are [they all],
> witlessly stumbling along.
> They [have turned] all their deeds to folly;
> they have become abhorrent unto themselves.
>
> . . . .
>
> Preachers of lies are they,
> prophets of deceit.
> They have plotted mischief against me,
> to make Thy people exchange for smooth words
> Thy teaching which Thou hast engraven on my heart.
>
> . . . .
>
> Crafty men are they;
> they think base thoughts,
> seek Thee with heart divided,
> stand not firm in Thy truth.
> In their every thought is a root
> which blossoms to wormwood and gall.
> In the stubbornness of their hearts
> they wander astray
> and go seeking thee through idols.[2]

Neither here nor in Matthew 23 are we in possession of the words of a neutral observer! One is aware that he is hearing only one side of the argument. In both the Gospel passage and the Hymn we see harsh overstatement. It is the language of conflict.

EARLY CHRISTIANS AND PHARISEES

Another approach to the attack on the Pharisees in Matthew 23 is to view it in terms of a later era. The hostility of this passage may reflect a period after the death and resurrection of Jesus, when Pharisaic opposition to Christians (see, e.g., Matt. 23:34) made it clear that they had rejected him as the Messiah. In this time of stormy confrontation with the Pharisees, Christians remembered Jesus' own conflict with them, and they sharpened his criticism of them. The Pharisees, to the early Christians, were no longer rivals who simply questioned and debated with Jesus. In the light of their rejection of the resurrected Christ, they came to be viewed as near demonic persons.

JUDAISM FOUNDED ON HYPOCRISY?

There is no reason to deny the Gospel witness that Jesus was in conflict with the Pharisees. Further, that there were some Pharisees who were insincere, should occasion no great surprise. People who made a pretense of religion were opposed by the prophets and the later rabbis.[3] The accusations made by the prophets, Jesus and the rabbis are not alien to us today. If these sins are represented, at the present time, in both the Jewish and Christian communities, most likely they were alive in an ancient day as well. But to make all, or most, Pharisees insincere is seriously to misrepresent the actual situation. Judaism would surely have died long ago if there had been such hollowness among the leaders who gave shape to its life and thought. But, as a matter of fact, it has continued with strength over nineteen hundred years, even in the face of repeated persecution. This truth encourages us to take a closer look at Pharisaic life-style and thought.

THE GOOD PHARISEES

Although there are a number of passages in the Gospels that portray the Pharisees as false and intolerant leaders, now and then, a more complimentary view emerges in the New Testament. A surprising reference to the Pharisees occurs in Luke 13:31. Some of them warned Jesus of Herod's intention to kill him and they urged him to hide and save himself! In the book of Acts (5:33-39), a Pharisee, named Gamaliel, is presented as the model of tolerance and fair-mindedness. He stood among a gathering of Jews listening to the apostles, who were witnessing of the death and resurrection of Jesus. The crowd was in an angry mood because of the apostles' accusation that they had killed Jesus. Before violence broke out, Gamaliel arose and calmed the people: " 'Keep away from these men and let them alone, for if this plan or this undertaking is of men it will fail; but if it is of God, you will not be able to overthrow them. You might even be found opposing God.' "

The Gamaliel mentioned in the above passage, appears to be the devout and influential Pharisaic leader referred to in the Mishnah.[4] Acts 22:3 refers to him as the teacher of the Apostle Paul. Significantly, Paul identifies himself as a Pharisee,[5] and although he offers criticism of their teaching, he never accuses them of insincerity.

DO WHAT THE PHARISEES TELL YOU

Surprisingly, Matthew 23:2-3 recognizes the validity of Pharisaic authority. Because this passage appears in the context of accusations against the Pharisees, it is often overlooked. The Gospel writer reports that Jesus spoke to a group of people, which included his own disciples, and said: " 'The scribes and the Pharisees sit on Moses' seat [i.e., they teach with the authority of Moses]; so practice and observe whatever they tell you.' "
In the light of the conflicts between Jesus and the Pharisees

which are described in the Gospels, these are astonishing words. They echo a genuine teaching of Jesus. Certainly no later Christian writer would have attributed these words to Jesus, if he had not spoken them at one time.

SHAKING FISTS AND SHAKING HANDS

What are we to make of these words in Matthew 23? One must not read too much into them but, on the other hand, such a statement should not be passed over lightly. At the very least, this text demonstrates that Jesus gave general approval to some aspects of Pharisaic teaching.[6] It informs us that Jesus and the Pharisees may not be viewed simply as opponents who regularly shake their fists at each other. The text helps us to understand the references in the Gospels to occasions when Jesus and the Pharisees ate together (e.g., Luke 14:1). If their relationship had been only a hostile one, it is not likely that they would have shared the intimacy of a meal.

JOSEPHUS AND THE PHARISEES

Besides their appearance in the New Testament, the Pharisees are mentioned with some frequency in the works of Josephus, a Jewish author who lived in the latter part of the first century A.D. He identifies himself as a follower of the Pharisees.[7] In agreement with the New Testament, he describes the Pharisees as men who excelled in religious observances and were experts in the matter of Law.[8] From his writings we also learn that they sought political power for themselves in order to propagate their teachings. When in possession of this power they could be quite ruthless in eliminating their opposition.[9]

THE PHARISEES ARE WELL-LIKED

But, if there are passages in Josephus that present the Pharisees as seekers after power, there are others that speak of them in very favorable terms. At one point in his writings, Josephus observes:

> The Pharisees are affectionate to each other and cultivate harmonious relations with the community. The Sadducees, on the contrary, are, even among themselves, rather boorish in their behaviour, and in their intercourse with their peers are as rude as to aliens.[10]

On another occasion it is stated: "The Pharisees simplify their standard of living, making no concessions to luxury." They are seen to be

> extremely influential among the townsfolk; and all prayers and sacred rites of divine worship are performed according to their exposition. This is the great tribute that the inhabitants of the cities, by practicing the highest ideals both in their way of living and in their discourses, have paid to the excellence of the Pharisees.[11]

In yet another passage, Josephus informs us that the influence of the Sadducees is limited to the wealthy, but "the Pharisees have the support of the masses."[12] Further, we learn that they are lenient in their recommendations of punishment for those who have committed misdeeds.[13]

In summary, we learn from Josephus that the ideals of the Pharisees are admired and that there is high regard for the way in which they live out their lives. They are people who excel in their religious life and who communicate genuineness to the common people. They live exemplary lives, get along with each other and bring about peace in their community.

WHO ARE THE PHARISEES?

In order to better appreciate the relationship that existed between Jesus and the Pharisees, we will summarize what may be known about their origin and thought. Neither in the Old Testament nor in pre-Christian Jewish literature are the Pharisees mentioned. As we have already observed, the first specific references to them come in the first century of the Christian era, in the writings of Josephus and the New Testament. By the time we meet them in this literature, it is evident that they are already a well-established movement. There are many theories about the rise of the Pharisees, but the evidence is sparse. One may not be dogmatic. However, the suggestion that their origin roots in the social and religious upheaval occurring about 170 B.C., has much to commend it.[14]

THE RISE OF THE PHARISEES

After 587 B.C., the Jews were ruled for centuries by foreign powers. Shortly after 200 B.C. the Jewish community fell under the domination of rulers (the Seleucids) who were bent on converting the Jews to Greek ways of life and thought. The pressure upon them was intense. A number of Jews threw over the historic faith and began to imitate the manners of the ruling nation. Those that would not capitulate were persecuted and often killed. Despite the severe penalties, many Jews remained faithful. Onias III, the High Priest, held firmly to the sacred traditions. However, it was not long before the devout Onias fell victim to the invasion of Greek thought. Advocates of Hellenism bribed their way to the High Priesthood. Onias III was deposed, exiled, and finally killed. The corruption of priestly leadership left the people without guidance and example. A threat of extinction faced the Jewish community unless others, committed to the tradition of the past, assumed leadership. The conjecture is that the people, who later became known as Pharisees,[15] moved into positions of authority in the community, revitalized Jewish piety and successfully checked the Hellenizers. Those whom we know as Sadducees are the descendants of the old priesthood whose collapse was the occasion for the rise of the Pharisees. Although the two movements shared many beliefs, they differed at important points as will be noted in the following pages.

MAKING RELIGION RELEVANT

The title "Pharisees" means "separated ones" and appears to refer to their separated way of living, which was in strict observance of the Law. From our sources, namely the New Testament and Josephus, we learn that these men were experts in the interpretation of the Law, and that they excelled beyond all others in observing the commandments. But, although they were firm advocates of obedience to the Law, they seem to have been characterized by a humane spirit as well as a sensitivity to what changing times meant for the practice of religion. They attempted to make the Law relevant to the day in which they lived. This emphasis placed them against the aristocratic, priestly, keep-things-as-they-have-been Sadducees, who advocated a more literal understanding of the Law. The Pharisees represented a progressive, democratic movement in Judaism. Among the common people they had a large following.

However, in spite of the fact that the common people held them in high honor, one should not think of them as a group of religious leaders who supported a relaxed attitude in religious observance. The fact that their name means "separated ones" probably points not only to their own exclusiveness, but also to the strict demands they made on those who followed them.[16] But their expectations were not unreasonable. Some laws in the Pentateuch, if taken literally, were too rigorous to obey, while others were out of touch with the life of the average person. These scholars re-interpreted those commandments so that the demands of the Law would be both humane and appealing to common sense.

THE UNWRITTEN LAW

What gave the Pharisees the right to reinterpret and update the ancient Law found in the Pentateuch? According to Josephus, they based their interpretations on traditions that had been passed on from generation to generation by word of mouth.[17] Reference is made to these traditions in the New Testament as well.[18] The Pharisees regarded the word-of-mouth traditions (often referred to as the Oral Law) to be authoritative whereas the Sadducees did not. The latter held that only the laws written in the Hebrew Bible were to be obeyed.

THE PHARISAIC INTERPRETATION OF THE LAW

Unfortunately, we have no examples of Pharisaic interpretation of Scripture that can be traced back, with certainty, to the time of the Pharisees. There is, however, a large body of later rabbinic writings, which represents the literary deposit of the Pharisaic tradition. This literature may give us some idea of the way the Pharisees approached the Law. With the above caution in mind, we will look at some rabbinic comments on the Law.

THE SABBATH IS FOR PEOPLE

The text recorded in Exodus 35:2 sounds a serious warning:

"Six days shall work be done, but on the seventh day you shall have a holy sabbath of solemn rest to the LORD; whoever does any work on it shall be put to death."

The sabbath broke the six day routine of community toil. It was a special time, a day set apart for God. On this day people were to do no work. However, the commandment gives no definition of "work." How is one to obey this law? What actions are allowed on the sabbath? Which ones are prohibited? The rabbis recognized the problem and took the responsibility for defining, in concrete terms, what constituted "work."

The main labours [prohibited on the Sabbath] are forty less one: sowing, ploughing, reaping, binding sheaves, threshing, winnowing, cleansing, grinding, sifting, kneading, baking, shearing the wool and washing or beating or dyeing it, spinning, weaving, making two loops, weaving two threads, separating two threads, tying a knot or loosening one, sewing two stitches, tearing in order to sew two stitches, hunting a deer and slaughtering it or flaying it or salting it or curing its skin or scraping it or cutting it up, writing two letters, erasing in order to write two letters, building, demolishing, extinguishing, kindling, striking with a hammer, carrying from one domain into another. These are the chief labours [forbidden on the Sabbath]—forty less one.[19]

A long list! It is difficult for us to react positively to these itemized sabbath proscriptions. They seem too rigid, too detailed. Yet, it should be observed that the things forbidden represent actions characteristic of a society at work. The activities listed are those that could be suspended for a day without any great inconvenience or danger to the community. The termination of work honored the sanctity of this day, and enabled persons to give themselves in corporate worship of God.

SUNDAY SABBATH LAWS

These restrictions are not as far removed from our day as we might think. It was not too long ago that a similar celebration of Sunday was in force. Under the Sunday Laws, of which many Christians approved, businesses and places of entertainment were forced to close for the day. Some Christian groups still advocate an observance of Sunday which, in the main, is attendance at Church services and rest at home. Shopping, travel, entertainment, play, and work are discouraged on this day. These views are still alive within the Christian Church some seventeen hundred years after the appearance of the above passage in the Mishnah. The motive for such prohibitions is admirable. As in the case of rabbinic restrictions concerning the sabbath, it is an attempt to make Sunday a special, holy day. In a recent issue of the *Reader's Digest,* Billy Graham, for that very reason, is suggesting a return to a more strict observance of the first day of the week.[20] In any case, let it be noted that the restrictions in the mishnaic passage were not nearly so limiting as the text of Scripture itself. If one followed the interpretation of the Pharisaic tradition, it meant that if the activity envisaged was not within the list of forbidden activities, one was free to do it.

HONOR AND ENJOY THE SABBATH

The intention of the Pharisaic interpretation was to keep proper respect for the sabbath while granting freedom to enjoy the day.[21] This purpose finds expression in the rabbinic understanding of Exodus 16:29 which commands: " 'Remain every man of you in his place, let no man go out of his place on the seventh day.' " From the context, the term "place" must mean one's home. In fact, the Septuagint, the Greek version of the Old Testament, translates "place" as "house." But, in the tradition passed on by the Pharisees, "place" came to mean one's city.[22] This meant that people had freedom to walk around and enjoy themselves on the sabbath. However, it was not a day on which one should plan a trip to another city, unless an emergency occasioned it. The Pharisaic interpretation tried to abide by the spirit of the Law. One should honor the sabbath as a day apart from other days, but it should not be a sad or dull day. One should enjoy it. After all, it was said, "The Sabbath is given to you but you are not surrendered to the Sabbath."[23]

COMPENSATION IS BETTER THAN RETALIATION

Exodus 21:23-24 lays down the law of " 'life for life, eye for eye, tooth for tooth, hand for hand, foot for foot, burn for burn, wound for wound, stripe for stripe.' " Although the impulse of retaliation is written deep in the human spirit, the brutal response of like for like was rejected in the Jewish community. The rabbis taught that compensation, not retaliation, was the appropriate response to the one who had been injured.[24]

LIMITING THE DEATH PENALTY

According to the Law, the son who is rebellious to his parents (Deut. 21:18f.) and strikes or curses them (Exod. 21:15; Lev. 20:9) may be executed. But the rabbis drew back from such a harsh penalty. They made certain that this law would almost never be enforced by surrounding it with numerous qualifications. Law was employed to modify the Law. For example, minors were exempt from punishment, both parents must be in agreement in the accusation against the son, the accused must be admonished before three judges and, if he were still rebellious, scourged before them. Finally, when the son is to be tried for the crime against his parents (after the above restrictions and others listed in the Mishnah are observed), he must appear before twenty-three judges who will give the verdict.[25]

THIS IS YOUR RESPONSIBLE SHARE

In Leviticus 19:9-10 and 23:22, farm owners are instructed to leave some of the harvest for the poor. However, the text does not say *how much* should be left. No doubt some people left very little. The imprecise character of the Law enabled the wealthy in the community to escape their responsibility. Aware of this, the rabbis declared that the amount of the harvest left behind should be in proportion to the size of the harvest. They ruled that the very least amount that one should leave behind was one-sixtieth of the full yield.[26] This teaching has a "legal" ring to it, but it speaks of love rather than legalistic red tape. The rabbis were convinced, that if the Law were to function it had to be specific. Out of consideration for the poor they established a minimum gift. They knew the heart of some people. If one says to these people, "you may give whatever you wish to this cause," they will give little or nothing. Thus the rabbis "helped" such people to be responsible! Though phrased in lawyer-like language, the basic concern of this interpretation of the Law is one that the prophets would certainly applaud.

AGREEMENT AND DISAGREEMENT

In Matthew 23:2-3, Jesus told his hearers that the Pharisees had the authority of Moses, and instructed them to " 'practice and observe whatever they tell you.' " Apparently Jesus agreed with the Pharisees in their general approach to Scripture. Both he and the Pharisees embraced an interpretation of the Law that was much more liberal than that of the Sadducees. However, in adopting this approach to the Law, one is faced with a question: when do freedom and flexibility in the interpretation of the Law undercut the whole structure of Law? The Pharisees and Jesus are in agreement that the Law needs interpretation. But the Pharisees take issue with Jesus. They believe he has adopted such a liberal interpretation of the Law that his teaching amounts to a rejection of Law itself. They fear the ambiguity of his position for they believe that religion must say something specific about how life is to be lived. A too general interpretation of the Law gives overmuch freedom and encourages irresponsible behavior. For his part, Jesus believes that, for all the good that may be found in the approach of the Pharisees, they emphasize too much a juristic interpretation (Mark 2:23ff.; 3:1ff.).

LIFE BEYOND DEATH

Belief in a life after death for the individual was a central conviction of the Pharisees, according to the testimony of both the New Testament and Josephus. The latter says of them:

> Every soul, they maintain, is imperishable, but the soul of the good alone passes into another body, while the souls of the wicked suffer eternal punishment.[27]

They believe that souls have power to survive death and that there are rewards and punishments under the earth for those who have led lives of virtue or vice: eternal imprisonment is the lot of evil souls, while the good souls receive an easy passage to a new life. Because of these views they are, as a matter of fact, extremely influential among the townsfolk. . . .[28]

This report of Josephus is confirmed by a passage in the book of Acts (23:8): "For the Sadducees say that there is no resurrection, nor angel nor spirit; but the Pharisees acknowledge them all."

The Sadducees, in their denial of the resurrection, represented the main stream of Old Testament thought, which was a national hope for peace and prosperity in this life. Generally, in the Hebrew Scriptures, hope for the individual, apart from the nation, is given little attention.[29] Although there may be some hints of life after death for the individual in a few Old Testament passages (e.g., Ps. 73:24), the only explicit reference to the individual's resurrection from the dead is found in the book of Daniel.[30]

PERSONAL RESURRECTION

In a time when life was precarious and there was little hope of national restoration, the Pharisaic witness of life after death was an attractive teaching. However, it is not a hope for careless or rebellious persons. Josephus, summarizing Pharisaic belief, declares that for those who

live in accordance with our laws [i.e., Pharisaic laws] the prize is not silver or gold, no crown of wild olive or of parsley with any such public mark of distinction. No; *each individual,* relying on the witness of his own conscience and the lawgiver's prophecy, confirmed by the sure testimony of God, is firmly persuaded that to *those who observe the laws* and, if they must needs die for them, willingly meet death, *God has granted a renewed existence* and the revolution of the ages the *gift of a better life.*[31]

One is assured of this "gift of a better life" *if* one is obedient
to the Law. How life is lived in the day by day world, deter-
mines one's eternal destiny. There are rewards for the righteous
and punishments for the wicked. Each person is responsible for
his or her own life.

THE SYNAGOGUE

Although the origins of the synagogue are somewhat
clouded, it is likely that it developed under the influence of
the Pharisees.[32] Because the leaders of the Synagogue (i.e., the
Pharisees) were scholars of the Law and not priests, significant change took place in Jewish worship. The Synagogue
gave no place to sacrifice, which was the prominent ritual of
the temple. Rather, at its center was prayer together with the
study and observance of the Law. Firmly established in Judaism by the Christian era, the Synagogue played an important
role in the survival of the Jewish community after the destruction of the temple in 70 A.D. It provided an alternative pattern
of life and worship.

CONVERTS TO JUDAISM

Josephus informs us about the popularity of Pharisaic leadership among the Jews. However, Pharisaic teaching did not
appeal only to Jews. Gentiles also found the Judaism of the
Pharisees to be a faith that spoke to the important issues of life.
Many associated with the Synagogue community and lived
their lives according to the traditions of the Jewish worshipers.
Others converted fully to Judaism. Not only did Judaism *receive* converts, but, according to Matthew 23:15, there was an
active missionary movement among the Pharisees. However, of
this program we have little information.

ERASING THE CARICATURES

The Pharisees may not be dismissed as hypocritical leaders of a near dead religion. Information coming from Josephus, the literature formed by the Pharisaic tradition (the Talmud) and even the New Testament, draws a different picture of these leaders. Although Pharisees are not above criticism, these sources help us to appreciate the quality of life and thought represented among them. They also give us a better understanding of what happened in the first Christian century. The fact that most Jews did not convert to Christianity (and relatively few have done so since) tells us something about the nature of Pharisaic Judaism. If these Jews had not found something genuine and nourishing in their faith, would they have remained Jews?

The differences which exist between the teachings of Jesus and those of the Pharisees should not be minimized. Nevertheless, it is important to recognize similarities, if we are to achieve a balanced view of the relationship between the two. The teaching of the Pharisees[33] concerning the law, resurrection, future judgment as well as the Pharisaic development of a non-sacrificial worship, provides ample proof that the Pharisees and Jesus were not totally at odds. Against the background of their teachings, the words which Jesus speaks about them to his hearers make sense: "so practice and observe whatever they tell you." The presence of these words in the Gospel of Matthew means that, although Jesus offered severe criticism of the Pharisees, he also had appreciation for the basic elements of their teaching. These words correct a long tradition within the Church. Too frequently we have only focused on the negative aspects of the Pharisaic movement, and have failed to give attention to those strengths that have attracted multitudes of Jews—and some Gentiles also.

NOTES

1. No doubt some of the references to the Pharisees in rabbinic literature derive from this same period. Although the Mishnah, for example, was not written down until about 200 A.D., it existed for a long time in oral form and therefore may contain "eyewitness" material. Generally, rabbinic sources agree with the description of the Pharisees given by Josephus. The difficulty in dating the rabbinic passages has led us to exclude them from consideration. Further, a number of scholars believe that the apocryphal book, Second Maccabees (1st century B.C.), shows acquaintance with the Pharisaic movement. However, because the term Pharisee never occurs in this material we have eliminated this book from our discussion also. For a good discussion of the problems involved in understanding the Pharisees, consult Jacob Neusner, *From Politics to Piety: The Emergence of Pharisaic Judaism* (Englewood Cliffs, New Jersey: Prentice-Hall, 1973).

2. Hymn 4:6ff. The translation is that of Theodor H. Gaster, *The Dead Sea Scriptures* (Garden City: Doubleday, 1956), pp. 142-143. David Flusser, *Jesus* translated by Ronald Walls (New York: Herder and Herder, 1969), p. 55 thinks these words are directed against the Pharisees. "A great deal of the anti-semitic imagery of the New Testament," says Jacob Agus, "is actually a reflection of sectarian Jewish thought and rhetoric." *Bulletin* of the Lutheran Theological Seminary, Gettysburg, Penn. (vol. 48, 1968) p. 42. Quoted by Franklin Sherman, *The Promise of Heschel* (New York: Lippincott Company, 1970), p. 73.

3. There are some passages in rabbinic literature which have been understood as denunciations of the Pharisees. However, this identification is not certain. Ellis Rivkin, "Defining the Pharisees: The Tannaitic Sources," *Hebrew Union College Annual* 40 (1969) 240-41, argues that these texts refer not to Pharisees but to religious extremists. Whether or not they are to be defined as Pharisees is not all that important for our purpose. These passages remind us that Jewish teachers, as all other sensitive men of faith, directed sharp criticism at those who make a show of religion. See Blackman, Sotah 3:4, pp. 347-48 (Order Nashim) and Epstein, Sotah 22b, pp. 112-13 (Seder Nashim). For other passages which condemn hypocrisy, see also Epstein, Sotah 41b and 42a, pp. 205-06 (Seder Nashim) and Yoma 86b, pp. 431-32 (Seder Mo'ed).

4. Blackman, Sotah 9:15, p. 382 (Order Nashim).

5. See Galatians 1:13 ff.; Philippians 3:5; Acts 23:1-10; Acts 26:5.

6. See also the agreement between Jesus and a scribe concerning which commandments are the most important (Mark 12:28-34). Scribes appear to be closely affiliated with the Pharisees.

7. *The Life,* volume 1, p. 7. "Being now in my nineteenth year I began to govern my life by the rule of the Pharisees, a sect having points of resemblance to that which the Greeks call the Stoic school." All refer-

ences to the text of *Josephus* are from the Loeb Classical Library edition of nine volumes, edited and translated by H. St. J. Thackeray, Ralph Marcus, Allen Wikgren and Louis H. Feldman. Vols. 1-4 (1926-30) published by G. P. Putnam's Sons in New York and William Heinemann in London. Vols. 5-9 (1934-1965) published by Harvard University Press in Cambridge, Mass. and William Heinemann in New York. Vols 8 and 9 © The President and Fellows of Harvard College, 1963, 1965.

8. *The Jewish War,* volume 2, p. 53. "Beside Alexandra, and growing as she grew, arose the Pharisees, a body of Jews with the reputation of excelling the rest of their nation in the observances of religion, and as exact opponents of the laws."

9. *The Jewish War,* volume 2, pp. 53-55; *Jewish Antiquities,* volume 7, pp. 431-35. See Jacob Neusner, *From Politics to Piety: The Emergence of Pharisaic Judaism* (Englewood Cliffs, New Jersey: Prentice-Hall, 1973), pp. 49-52.

10. *The Jewish War,* volume 2, p. 387.

11. *Jewish Antiquities,* volume 9, pp. 11-13.

12. *Jewish Antiquities,* volume 7, p. 377. ". . . the Sadducees having the confidence of the wealthy alone but no following among the populace, while the Pharisees have the support of the masses."

13. *Jewish Antiquities,* volume 7, p. 377. ". . . the Pharisees are naturally lenient in the matter of punishments."

14. This is the theory advanced by Ellis Rivkin, *The Shaping of Jewish History* (New York: Scribner's Sons, 1971), pp. 42-83. See also his essay, "The Pharisaic Background of Christianity," in *Root and Branch: The Jewish-Christian Dialogue* edited by Michael Zeik and Martin Siegel (New York: Roth Publishing, 1973), pp. 47-70.

15. In *Jewish Antiquities,* volume 7, pp. 373-79, Josephus informs us that the Pharisees constituted a significant party in the time of John Hyrcanus, who assumed power in 134 B.C. Although they must have existed before this period, we have no explicit reference to their activity in an earlier era.

16. See Jakob Josef Petuchowski, *Heirs of the Pharisees* (New York: Basic Books, Inc., 1970), pp. 10ff.

17. *Jewish Antiquities,* volume 7, p. 377. "For the present I wish merely to explain that the Pharisees had passed on to the people certain regulations handed down by former generations and not recorded in the Laws of Moses, for which reason they are rejected by the Sadducean group, who hold that only those regulations should be considered valid which were written down (in Scripture), and that those which had been handed down by former generations need not be observed. And concerning these matters the two parties came to have controversies and serious differences, the Sadducees having the confidence of the wealthy alone but no following among the populace, while the Pharisees have the support of the masses." See the discussion of these "regulations

handed down" (i.e., the Oral Law) in Rivkin, *The Shaping of Jewish History*, pp. 50ff.

18. Galatians 1:14 and Matthew 15:1ff.
19. Blackman, Shabbath 7:2, p. 44 (Order Mo'ed). On the observance of the sabbath see the discussion of George Foot Moore, *Judaism in the First Centuries of the Christian Era*, II (Cambridge, Mass.: Harvard University Press, 1927), pp. 21-29.
20. Billy Graham, "Whatever Happened to the Old-Fashioned Sabbath?" *Reader's Digest* (January 1974) 99-101.
21. However, some later rabbis detailed even further these thirty-nine restrictions so that one ended up with 1521 classes of prohibited work. See Moore, *Judaism* II, p. 28. When religion becomes entwined in such detail it no longer creates freedom. It becomes burdensome. But such an extreme view of sabbath observances was not characteristic of rabbinic teaching. Every religion, Christianity no less than Judaism, is afflicted by extremists. It is unfair to evaluate a faith in terms of its excess.
22. Epstein, 'Erubin 51a, p. 353 (Seder Mo'ed).
23. Lauterbach, vol. 3, p. 198 (Shabbata, Exod. 31:12-17).
24. Epstein, Baba Kamma 83b, pp. 473-477 (Seder Nezikin).
25. Blackman, Sanhedrin 8:1-5, pp. 274-78 (Order Nezikin). See the discussion of G. F. Moore, *Judaism* II, pp. 134-35.
26. Blackman, Pe'ah 1:2, p. 83 (Order Zera'im).
27. *The Jewish War*, volume 2, pp. 385-86.
28. *Jewish Antiquities*, volume 9, p. 13.
29. However, compare Deuteronomy 24:16, Jeremiah 31:29-30 and Ezekiel 18:1-28.
30. Daniel 12:2-3.
31. *Against Apion*, volume 1, p. 381. See Rivkin's fine discussion in *The Shaping of Jewish History*, 53 ff.
32. See Rivkin, "The Pharisaic Background to Christianity," *Root and Branch*, p. 65.
33. Pharisaic teaching included much more than we have indicated in our brief discussion. Acts 23:8 indicates that they believed in spirit and angels. Josephus declares that fate as well as belief in human freedom were a part of their thought also. *Jewish Antiquities*, volume 9, pp. 11-13.

FOR FURTHER READING

Coleman, William. *Those Pharisees*. New York: Hawthorn Books, Inc., 1977. The author demonstrates that a Christian, who is sensitive to life in the Christian community, will find little difficulty in understanding the problems and solutions of the Pharisees. For the layperson.

Cook, Michael. "Jesus and the Pharisees: The Problem as It Stands Today," in *Journal of Ecumenical Studies.* To appear in 1978 or 1979.

Davies, W. D. *Introduction to Pharisaism.* Philadelphia: Fortress Press, 1967. Brief (32 pages), but excellent introduction.

Finkelstein, Louis. *The Pharisees: The Sociological Background of Their Faith,* I-II. Philadelphia: The Jewish Publication Society, 1938. Although an older book, its contribution to the study of the Pharisees is highly valued.

Herford, R. Travers. *The Pharisees.* New York: Macmillan, 1924. Although old, it contains much helpful material on the Pharisees and Judaism in general.

Moore, George F. *Judaism in the First Centuries of the Christian Era,* I-II. Cambridge, Mass.: Harvard University Press, 1927. Pp. 56-121. A universally respected scholar who opened up rabbinic literature to both Jew and Christian. Although some of his judgments need revision in terms of new investigation, these volumes may be read with profit.

Neusner, Jacob. *From Politics to Piety: The Emergence of Pharisaic Judaism.* Englewood Cliffs, New Jersey: Prentice-Hall, 1973. Paper. The author has written voluminously on Pharisaic-rabbinical thought. He is one of the acknowledged leaders in this area today. Not the easiest of readings but rewarding for the one who perseveres!

Parkes, James. *The Foundations of Judaism and Christianity.* Chicago: Quadrangle, 1960. Dr. Parkes has labored for years to bring about better understanding between Jews and Christians. His comments on the Pharisees may be found in various sections of his book. A most sympathetic presentation of Pharisaic teaching.

Petuchowski, Jakob J. *Heirs of the Pharisees.* New York: Basic Books, Inc., 1970. Paper. The book is a series of essays which have been published in similar form elsewhere. The first chapter, "The Pharisaic Tradition Today," will be of special interest to the reader.

Phipps, William. "Jesus, the Prophetic Pharisee," in *Journal of Ecumenical Studies* (1977), 17-31. An excellent article which investigates the portrayal of Jesus in the Synoptic Gospels. On the basis of this material he believes that Jesus belonged to the Pharisaic tradition even though at some points he differed with the Pharisees.

Rivkin, Ellis. *The Shaping of Jewish History: A Radical New Interpretation.* New York: Scribner's Sons, 1971. An important book by one who considers the Pharisees to be the revolutionaries of their day. The "Pharisaic Revolution" (Chapter 3), in his opinion both "saved" Judaism and gave rise to Christianity. Well written.

Rivkin, Ellis. "The Pharisaic Background of Christianity" in *Root and Branch: The Jewish-Christian Dialogue* (eds., Michael Zeik and Martin Siegel). Williston Park, New York: Roth Publishing, 1973. Paper represents the view stated above. Excellent presentation.

Rivkin, Ellis. "Pharisees," in *Interpreter's Dictionary of the Bible,* Supplementary Volume. New York: Abingdon, 1976.

Chapter Nine

THE CHARACTER
OF
MODERN JUDAISM

As the Cross dominates the sanctuaries of Christian
Churches so the Ark, an upright chest which houses the Torah
scroll, is the most conspicuous object in the Synagogue.
Located at the front, its ornate decoration immediately attracts
the eye as one enters for worship. At an appointed time in the
service, the scroll is reverently removed from the Ark and
placed on the reading desk. Following the reading of a selection
from the scroll, a prayer of thanksgiving, similar to the following is offered:

> Blessed is the Lord our God, Ruler of the universe, who has given
> us a Torah of truth, implanting within us eternal life. Blessed is
> the Lord, Giver of Torah.[1]

The Torah scroll (that is, the Pentateuch) is the "heart of
Judaism," declares Lionel Blue, a Reform rabbi in England. He
asks one to think of a "cross-section of a tree. The innermost
ring is the Torah—the teaching, the Law—and around it clus-
ter ring after ring of commentary and argument, as each generation adds its own life experience to the formative experience of
the people."[2] This scroll tells the story of Israel's beginnings
with God and records the commandments which he gave to
her. For these reasons it holds the place of honor in the Jewish
tradition. But Torah is not limited to the first five books of the
Bible; it pervades the whole Old Testament. For example, the

prophets are men of Torah. These exceptional men did not introduce novel ideas to Israel, rather, they called people back to those teachings of Torah that formed the basis of Israel's ancient covenant with God. The later rabbis, together with the prophets and psalmists, were also men of Torah. The Talmud, which represents the teaching of these men, has one great concern: the understanding of Torah.

TORAH: A FULFILLING WAY OF LIFE

In the preceding chapters we observed that the Torah with its varied commandments is viewed as a divine gift to the Israelite community. It reveals God's way of life for the people he created. The commandments are not seen as arbitrary rules dispensed by a divine tyrant who wanted everyone to do things his way. No, the witness of Scripture is that these commandments arose out of a loving relationship that God had formed with Israel in the Exodus. They reveal God's caring concern for his people. The Torah points Israel to a full and fulfilling way of life.

DOWN-TO-EARTH TEACHING

Further, the discussion in previous chapters has shown that the commandments of the Torah are concerned with "everyday people" who daily are called upon to make numerous decisions as to what they should and should not do. The Torah has a very practical character. The focus is not upon abstract ideas of Good and Evil but upon good and evil acts. Many religions set up high ideals for people but fail to give practical instruction as to how these ideals are to be expressed in the daily routine of life. For the most part, Judaism is exempted from this criticism because the Torah addresses itself to every area of life in this world. For example, it speaks to family relationships, social and business contacts, celebration of sacred days, foods to be eaten, inheritance, marriage, and divorce. The Torah is down-to-earth instruction on how to act.[3] The deed is of first importance. Torah defines Judaism as a way of living in this world.

JUDAISM THROUGH THE EYES OF HESCHEL

Modern Judaism is the focus of the present chapter. More specifically, the following pages attempt to answer the question: *what is the character of a religion whose "heart" is Torah (Law)?* However, we face some difficulty in confronting this question. Present-day Judaism falls into three main divisions: Orthodox, Conservative, and Reform. These groups vary considerably in their understanding of the commandments of the Torah and their validity for today's world. It is not possible to represent fairly these various positions in the brief discussion that follows. For this reason I have chosen to view modern Judaism through the eyes of Abraham Joshua Heschel who has written passionately and extensively on the above subject. Although he died in 1972, through his writings, he remains a front-ranking figure in Judaism today.[4] His views are not those of all Jews. However, as much as any one person can, he represents the "center flow" of Jewish thinking.

TORAH: GOD REACHING OUT

Israel owed her existence to the God who acted on her behalf. God sought her. God is seeking us today. "All of human history as described in the Bible," declares Heschel, "may be summarized in one phrase: *God is in search of man.* "[5] True, the Bible speaks of people seeking God. But when we "find" God, it is because he has been searching for us. Heschel is impatient with religious thinkers who conceive of God as some unfeeling object "up there" waiting to be found. A God whom we must find cannot be much interested in us. Even if one proves his existence, what good is that? He will still sit in his heaven at a divine distance from our world. Such a God is alien to Judaism. The Exodus and Sinai events proclaim a God who is in search of human beings. Out of deep concern for people, he reaches out and encourages their search after him.

THE GOD OF PATHOS

It is this concern of God for people that involves him in an "emotional" relationship with the world. He is affected by what he sees happening on the human scene. Joy or sorrow, anger or grief grasp him as he views the conduct of the people he created. He is a God of pathos. Heschel defines the pathos of God as a "living care" for humanity, or as a "dynamic relation between God and man."[6]

TO ACT OR NOT TO ACT IS THE ISSUE

The *deed* is the focus of God's pathos. It is not primarily what people *intend* to do or *think* about that causes God joy or grief, but what people *actually do* to each other. What one intends to do (i.e., if it remains only an intention) scarcely hurts or helps anyone. On the other hand, what one concretely does to others, leaves deep wounds and lasting scars, or brings healing and joy. The prophets, mirroring God's feelings about the way life is being lived, condemn *acts* of injustice and meanness. As faithful interpreters of Torah they point their hearers to *deeds* of love, justice, and faithfulness (see, e.g., Isa. 1:16).

TO BE A REMINDER OF GOD

The doing of justice and mercy (and refraining from doing evil) is an imitation of God himself, who by a divine act of kindness brought Israel into being (Mic. 6:3-8).[7] Israel was not saved by some great thought of God, but by an act of love that rescued her from Egypt. "What is the mission of man," asks

Heschel, "according to the Jewish view? To be a reminder of God! As God is compassionate, let man be compassionate. As God strives for meaning and justice, let man strive for meaning and justice."[8] It is in the act that we become reminders of God. Further, by means of the act we enter into fellowship and partnership with God. Heschel emphasizes that we can never know God as he truly is. We can only know him in his actions of love, power, judgment, salvation, and so on. This means that we most fully experience God when we cooperate with him in acts that reflect his will in life.

A LEAP OF ACTION

It is against the background of the preceding discussion that we should understand the following phrase coined by Heschel: "leap of action." The phrase belongs to Abraham Heschel, but its basic meaning is shared by Jews of every age. To know and experience God's presence, one must take a "leap of action" as well as a leap of thought or faith. For many of us this is an unusual approach, because we tend to think, as he says, that

> religion is a state of the soul, inwardness; feeling rather than obedience, faith rather than action, spiritual rather than concrete. To Judaism, religion is not a feeling for something that is, but *an answer* to Him who is asking us to live in a certain way.[9]

BELIEVE IN YOUR HEART

Naturally Heschel recognizes that religion must have an inward aspect. "No religious act is properly fulfilled unless it is done with a willing heart and a craving soul. You cannot worship Him with your body, if you do not know how to worship Him in your soul."[10] True religion must be more than the external act. It must be rooted deep in the heart of each person. But a commitment to God that occurs in the heart alone is not enough. Right *intention*, good *thoughts*, pious *feelings* are in the end nothing, if there is no act. God is a God of action and one does not meet him in thoughts or feelings. He is met when thoughts and acts become one.

MORE THAN INWARD RELIGION IS NEEDED

The prophets served as critics of an age that had largely ignored the Torah. People professed great love for God, rejoiced in his past favors and performed the necessary rituals— but they did not do justice. Their faith did not translate itself into faithful action. The conflict that the prophets had in their day is not very different from the struggle that prophetic figures have had in every age. The ready temptation for all people is to make religion spiritual, to locate it within the heart. But the important issue in religion, says Heschel, is right living in this world.

> The world needs more than the secret holiness of individual inwardness. It needs more than sacred sentiments and good intentions. God asks for the heart because He needs the lives. It is by lives that the world will be redeemed, by lives that beat in concordance with God, by deeds that outbeat the finite charity of the human heart.[11]

The inward is important; intention and right motives have their place, but to emphasize the spiritual overmuch is to affirm a half-truth.

CAN THE DEED CREATE FAITH?

Everyone agrees that deeds follow the intention of the heart. But, Heschel maintains, sometimes intention may follow the performance of the deed! "There is a way that leads *from* [acts of] *piety to faith.*"[12] It is true that one can perform religious acts without faith, but kind deeds may be a way of attaining and nourishing faith. "By living as Jews we may attain our faith as

Jews. We do not have faith because of deeds; we may attain faith through sacred deeds."[13]

BEING A PARTNER WITH GOD

When Jews do the commandments given by God, the opportunity of experiencing the divine presence offers itself. The deeds that are done may become deeds performed, not alone, but in partnership with God. In the performance of these good acts, which have the character of justice and kindness, one's own soul may be transformed as he seeks *"to be* what he *does."* [14] Doing good deeds is "catching." When one sees how such acts help, nourish, and give joy to others as well as to oneself, one wants to perform them. These acts are a

challenge to the soul. Indeed, one must be deliberately callous to remain forever deaf to the spirit of the acts he is engaged in performing day after day, year after year. How else can one learn the joy of loving-kindness, if not by enacting it?[15]

HEART AND ACT MUST BE ONE

The act teaches the soul. Thus, for example, should one who wishes to be an upright person engage continually in evil action, that person will become what he or she does and will become within and without an evil person. Similarly, if one gives oneself to the doing of good deeds, there is a good chance that the individual will ultimately become a good person. Heart and deed will sing the same song. This is the goal of Judaism.[16]

In summary, good deeds may lead to inner devotion, in which one becomes fully aware that one is a partner with God in bringing redemption to this world. In a manner similar to the prophets, one begins to feel the feelings of God and seeks to be a reminder of God in this world. One becomes a reminder of this God by imitating the gracious acts he performed for the benefit of Israel.

BY FAITH . . . BY DEED

The double theme of deed and faith has generated considerable discussion between Jews and Christians. Although there does exist a difference of opinion between the two communities, the variance is not as great as is sometimes imagined.

At first sight, the Apostle Paul's declaration on the subject appears clear. In several celebrated passages, he declares that one is "justified by faith apart from works of law." (Rom. 3:28) As an illustration of this principle, he refers to Abraham who was saved by faith before the Law was ever given (Gal. 3:6-29). However, Paul's strong emphasis on conduct should not be overlooked. The one "justified by faith" is to avoid immorality, impurity, licentiousness, idolatry, sorcery, enmity, selfishness, envy, and the like. The person who does these things is not a citizen of the kingdom of God. Those who belong to the kingdom are the people guided by the Spirit of God. Their conduct is characterized by love, joy, peace, patience, and other similar virtues (see Gal. 5:16-26).

WITHOUT FAITH . . . WITHOUT WORKS

In any discussion on this subject, the book of James deserves attention, for it makes plain that faith and works (deeds) are a totality. Paul had used Abraham as an example of one who had been saved by faith. James, on the other hand, employs Abraham as an illustration of one who was saved by works. True, James goes on to say that faith was active in Abraham's works. Nevertheless, the fact that he approaches the issue in this manner, suggests that he was opposing some people of his day who adhered to a "by faith alone" doctrine. Perhaps these people had misunderstood Paul. The book of James may even have been written to give some balance to Paul's teaching. At any rate, James concludes: "You see that a man is justified by works and not by faith alone." (James 2:24) His final word on this subject leaves no doubt about his position: "faith apart from works is dead." (James 2:26) The one cannot exist without the other.

A DIFFERENCE OF EMPHASIS

Both Jewish and Christian scholars would agree with James. The difference between the two communities is not at this point. The variance appears to be in the emphasis given to one aspect or the other. For example, Christian thought gives priority to faith which is to be completed by deeds. Heschel, and Judaism generally, would stress deeds through which faith is created and nourished. Both approaches have dangers. To emphasize faith overmuch may create the impression that religion is only inward feeling or belief. The strong opposition within the Church to social justice, indicates that a sizable group of Christians have succumbed to the temptation of making religion inward and personal. Jim Wallis, a young evangelical, makes this point in a recent book:

> The common failing of many evangelistic proclamations comes when there is a concentration upon getting one's heart right with God, which predominates over a primary concern for the meaning and coming of the kingdom. Christ the atoning sacrifice for sins is stressed to the exclusion of Christ the bringer and bearer of a new order in history that is in radical contradiction to the standards and structures of the present world.[17]

But the danger associated with an overemphasis on deeds is also real. Religion may become an impersonal legalism which lacks "heart." This hazard is not unknown to Heschel!

> Through sheer punctiliousness in observing the law one may become oblivious of the living presence and forget that the law is not for its own sake but for the sake of God. Indeed, the essence of observance has, at times, become encrusted with so many customs and conventions that the jewel was lost in the setting. Outward compliance with externalities of the law took the place of the engagement of the whole person to the living God. What is the

ultimate objective of observance if not to become sensitive to the spirit of Him, in whose ways the mitsvot [commandments] are signposts?[18]

That the Jewish and Christian communities have failed to keep good balance between faith and deeds, must be evident to any critic of the two faiths. Yet it should not be overlooked that life has been immeasurably enriched by a vast number of persons from both groups, who have put heart and deed together in a beautiful hymn of praise to God. In any discussion of differences between the two communities this joint contribution to life should not be forgotten.

PEOPLE ARE IMPORTANT

Who are we? Judaism places a high value on humanity. It is to us, not to the angels, that God revealed his will in the gift of the Torah. God trusted people to fulfill his Law![19]

The biblical narrative presents humankind created in the image of God, but made out of dust. The human being is "a vision of God and a mountain of dust. It is because of his being dust that his iniquities may be forgiven, and it is because of his being an image that his righteousness is expected."[20] The human is an in-between being. He stands just short of divinity, but is higher than the world of nature and animals. Within him there is desire for God, but also a pull toward the animal world. "He is the knot in which heaven and earth are interlaced."[21]

The insignificance of human beings in this mysterious universe is often emphasized. However, the biblical writings do not focus on our smallness, but on our unique ability to hear and serve God. "Man is man not because of what he has in common with the earth, but *because of what he has in common with God.* The Greek thinkers sought to understand man as *a part of the universe;* the prophets sought to understand man as *a partner of God.* "[22] Mankind is defined by his relationship to God. When the Bible speaks about humankind being created in the image of God, says Heschel, it is referring to his unique relationship to God. With a smile, Heschel observes that God broke his own law when he created humankind. The law states that one should not make anything in the likeness of heaven above (Exod. 20:4), yet God himself created humankind in the image of himself!

Human beings count for something with God. They are important! Though imperfect and inclined to sin, they are intended to be God's partner in the redemption of the world. The partnership is not a presumption on our part; it is the way God has structured life. It is the destiny that God has set for humanity. We are to strive to actually be what we were meant to be, namely, God's partner.

GOD NEEDS PEOPLE

God does very little without the partnership of humankind. He needs this "almost divine creature" to accomplish his will in the world, declares Heschel.

> There is a partnership of God and man. God needs our help. I would define man as a divine need. God is in need of man. In history, He cannot do the job alone . . . And the whole hope of messianic redemption depends on God and on man. We must help Him. And by each deed we carry out, we either retard or accelerate the coming of redemption. Our role in history is tremendous. I mean, our human role.[23]

These words illustrate the practical, descriptive character of Jewish thought. The above statement simply recognizes how things get done in the world. How does God help the poor, the sick, the bereaved, the hungry, and the oppressed in any community? Does he not aid them through people who love him. When there is mercy and justice in a community, is it not so because there are people present who have recognized their partnership with God? When harshness and injustice stretch a dark shadow across life, is it not due to a people's failure to respond to their divine Partner?

WHERE WAS GOD? . . . WHERE WAS HUMANKIND?

History overflows with cruelty and suffering. One asks the ancient question: why does God allow such suffering in his world? In our day that painful "why God" is asked repeatedly of Auschwitz. The murder of six million Jews by the Nazis is an inconceivable terror. Where was God? How could he allow the long lines to move slowly, but irresistibly, to the gas chambers and machine gun pits? Frightened people with uncomprehending children calling out for his help! He did not answer them. Where *was* God? Yes, it is a valid question, but one which should not be answered too quickly. Jewish tradition does not stop with that question. It also asks the practical question: where was humankind? Where was God's partner in the redemption of this world?

The history of the 1940s would have been different, if significant numbers of people had actually been what they were intended to be, God's partner in the everyday world. The Holocaust would not have happened if people had been responsible and concerned about being reminders of God in life. Where people cared, where people shared God's love for others, Jews were rescued. Naturally Jews were killed where people hated. But Jews were killed by apathy also, because this attitude allowed the executions to continue. God cannot do much when people do not care. Where human help was absent, people died. God cannot truly be God, in the running of this world, unless he has the cooperation of people. He failed to respond to six million pleas for deliverance because people did not care. He could not answer these crys for help because he had so few human partners.

DO IT SOMEHOW GOD!

During World War II I remember attending prayer meetings in which people would place before God the terrible suffering which was present in the world. From time to time the person offering prayer would ask God "to somehow" bring an end to such pain. But God could not do this by himself. He does not have some secret "somehow" which he can call upon in times of special distress. The "somehow" is a human being. The suffering inflicted upon one group of people by another can only end when God has the help of the creature he has created.

GOD ALWAYS CARES, BUT . . .

Heschel is at one with Jewish tradition in his insistence that people are responsible, with God, for what happens in this world. This is not a theoretical or speculative statement. It does not represent any attempt to state what God is in himself. Rather, it is a practical truth borne out by observing history. In the everyday world, God's love is made known by loving people. His justice, is reflected in just persons. When people forget who they are and become uncaring, God's care is hidden —even though God always cares. Heschel comments in one of his writings, that when persons are uncaring, God cares all the more! But, if people do not carry this love in their hearts, the divine kindness will not be effectively shared with the world.

People will continue to voice the question: where is God? Response will be varied. Some will find relief in affirming the mysterious hiddenness of God. Others will deny God's existence. Fully satisfying answers are difficult to find. Heschel's emphasis on a partnership between humankind and God presents a practical approach to certain kinds of suffering in our world. We cannot make God alone responsible for all the darkness in human life, because *we* are here. God has destined us to work "together" with him. We must strive to bring about the rule of God on earth. To forsake this responsibility, and to imagine that God will work his will without us, means that evil will continue to win and the rule of God will remain future. God cannot redeem this world without the aid of persons. God *needs* people. He cannot fully be God without the cooperation of his partner.

CAN WE DO THE WILL OF GOD?

But is humankind able to measure up to the awesome responsibility placed upon him by God? Yes, responds Heschel,

Judaism assumes that man is endowed with the ability to fulfill what God demands, at least to some degree. This may, indeed, be an article of prophetic faith: the belief in our ability to do His will. . . . Man's actual failures rather than his essential inability to do the good are constantly stressed by Jewish tradition.[24]

ORIGINAL SIN

Heschel recognizes that there is in the human heart a strong inclination toward sin. But, in distinction from Christianity, Judaism has never developed a doctrine of original sin. Although there is an awareness of a radical evil in the world, Jewish thinkers have not resorted to this doctrine to explain its presence in life. Adam's sin was not seen as an act that drastically altered the relationship between God and humankind. There is no thought that the sin of the first couple meant infection for the whole human race. "Jewish consciousness is not aware that the soul is buried under a curse or trapped by inherited guilt from which it must be saved."[25] Although an early Jewish writing[26] speaks of Adam's sin in terms reminiscent of St. Paul in Galatians and Romans, this view did not establish itself in later Judaism. The following comment by Heschel represents traditional Jewish thought on the subject of sin.

Though the Jewish view of life also embraces the profound consciousness of sin, it focuses on sin in a concrete sense, as a personal act committed against the will of a personal Creator. And though the sins may be grave and many, the evil done is not irremediable. The Christian reference to an ineradicable and comprehensive sinfulness in the nature of every man can never strike root in the Jewish mind. A mighty evil impulse there is in him, but in opposition to it there is also the good impulse.[27]

THE INCLINATION TO SIN

Heschel's discussion of evil is another reminder of the practical, realistic aspect of Jewish thought. The problem of evil in a universe created by God presses upon the mind. It is an enigma that Heschel does not ignore. He sees it as a puzzle that defies solution. But he lives in confidence that ultimately God will bring to an end the demonic in life. In harmony with Jewish tradition he does not focus on evil as a philosophical problem. Rather he emphasizes evil *acts* which individuals commit day by day.[28] An evil inclination seems present in all people. Everyone commits evil deeds.

WE NEED NOT SIN

The inclination to evil is strong, and too often it rules our actions. However, it need not dominate us. The fact that God entered into covenant with Israel at Sinai, and gave her the Law (after Adam's "Fall"), indicates that he had confidence in her ability to respond and obey the commandments. Deuteronomy 30:11-14 is clear on this point:

"For this commandment which I command you this day *is not too hard for you* [my emphasis], neither is it far off. It is not in heaven, that you should say, 'Who will go up for us to heaven, and bring it to us, that we may hear it and do it?' Neither is it beyond the sea, that you should say, 'Who will go over the sea for us, and bring it to us, that we may hear it and do it?' But the word is very near you; it is in your mouth and in your heart, so that you can do it."

The covenant at Sinai assumes that there is a Good Inclination within humankind. This inclination for the good is strengthened by the covenant relationship in which God becomes the partner of people in the doing of the commandments. God calls upon Israel to do his will which is revealed in the Law. But, it is important to keep in mind that the summons to obey does not come from some alien deity. The divine voice that addresses us, commanding obedience, is the voice of the Covenant-Partner who, in love, sought us out. The commands of this loving God not only instruct us as to what we should do, they give us strength to perform them. We are commanded therefore we can do them.[29]

> The Biblical answer to evil is not the good but the *holy*. It is an attempt to raise man to a higher level of existence, where man is not alone when confronted with evil. Living in "the light of the face of God" bestows upon man a power of love that enables him to overcome the powers of evil. The seductiveness of vice is excelled by the joys of the mitsvah [the good deed]. "Ye shall be men of holiness unto Me" (Exodus 22:30). How do we receive that quality, that power? "With every new mitsvah [good deed] which God issues to Israel, he adds holiness to them."[30]

THE LAW WILL HELP US

If one is tempted to do an evil act, let that person obey the Law for "obedience to the law prevents evil deeds."[31] In opposition to a view that has had long life in the Christian Church, Judaism holds that the Law is not a curse, but a blessing. It places no heavy burdens on the pious person. Rather it gives one strength to overcome evil acts. It is an "antidote" to evil.[32]

WE DO SIN BUT THERE IS FORGIVENESS

People are able to do the commandments, but as a matter of fact they often fail to observe them. No one is free of sin. God knows, however, that we are frail. Where there is repentance he forgives our sin. But, of course, it is never a matter of doing the commandments perfectly. No human being is capable of such excellence. With divine generosity God accepts our imperfect obedience of the commandments. Although the performance of the deed may have been deficient, the fact that it was done at all may witness to a heart seeking after God.

In the world of Jewish piety two voices may be heard. One voice is severe, uncompromising: good deeds done of impure motives are entirely inadequate. The other voice is one of moderation: good deeds are precious even if their motivation is not pure.

What are the facts? Even the finest intention is not strong enough to fill all corners of the soul which at all sides is open to intrusions of the ego. Judged by the severe, uncompromising standard of total purity of intention, who could stand? It is indeed, the voice of moderation that has generally prevailed. Thus we are taught to believe that "alien thoughts" or even improper motives do not vitiate the value of a sacred deed.

The soul is frail, but God is full of compassion for the distress of the soul, for the failure of the heart.[33]

The above views offer no comfort to superficial or insincere persons. Perfection is not demanded (that is reserved for God!), but it is expected that one will continue his attempt to obey the commandments so that, more and more, act and intention become one. The goal is to have the Law written on the heart.[34]

ACCENT ON THE POSITIVE

Although fully aware of humanity's inclination to sinful acts, Judaism has never centered attention upon the sinfulness of humanity. This is not to say that the presence of evil is an insignificant item in the life of humankind! But if one looks too long at the sinfulness of people, if one stresses too much the inability of people to do something good, the result may well be a shrug of the shoulders, which says simply, why try? If evil is so powerful in this world, if humanity is "fallen," if every aspect of life is twisted by evil, if we are unable to perform the

commandments which a loving God has given us to do, then,
it is argued, there can be little hope about this life. But Judaism
does have hope for our everyday world!

> The idea with which Judaism starts is not the realness of evil
> or the sinfulness of man [however, these realities are not denied
> in Judaism] but rather the wonder of creation and the ability of
> man to do the will of God. There is always opportunity to do a
> mitsvah [i.e., a good act], and precious is life because at all times
> and in all places we are able to do His will. *This is why despair is
> alien to Jewish faith.* [35]

THE REDEMPTION OF THIS WORLD

The Nazi Horror has caused many people to look again at
the nature of this world and humankind. Some who were once
optimistic are no longer. But Heschel and most present-day
Jewish thinkers have continued the realistic optimism long associated with Judaism. In Jewish tradition, humankind is still
the partner that God needs to bring about the redemption of
this world. "The world is in need of redemption, but the redemption must not be expected to happen as an act of sheer
grace. Man's task is to make the world worthy of redemption.
His faith and his works are preparations for *ultimate redemption.* "[36]

Judaism is committed to this life. The emphasis on deeds
and upon humanity as a partner with God, underline this commitment. There is an insistence that redemption must take
place in this world, which God has created, or it will not happen
at all. God must "prove" himself victor over evil in this life if
he is truly to be God. He is unable to bring about redemption
himself. He needs the cooperation of humankind. "We [Jews]
are God's stake in human history. . . . We carry the gold of God
in our souls to forge the gate of the kingdom."[37] When the
redemption comes it will have the character envisioned by the
prophets. God will rule in the hearts of people and they will
respond to each other in love.

THE LIFE TO COME

Judaism's commitment to this world does not exclude belief in the world to come. Jewish teaching stresses the importance of both worlds. The following statement from the Mishnah states it plainly, even if somewhat paradoxically:

> R. Jacob said: This world is like a vestibule before the world to come: prepare thyself in the vestibule that thou mayest enter into the banqueting hall.
>
> . . . Better is one hour of repentance and good works in this world than the whole life of the world to come; and better is one hour of bliss in the world to come than the whole life of this world.[38]

A number of present-day Jews reject the idea of personal resurrection or immortality and think instead of the dead as living on in their children. However, belief in life after death has deep roots in the Jewish religious tradition.[39] It represents an important affirmation even though there is little speculation concerning it in Jewish literature. Heschel was once asked why he had not written more about life beyond death. His answer is typically Jewish: "We believe in an afterlife. But we have no information about it. I think that's God's business what to do with me after life. Here it's my business what to do with my life. So I leave it to Him."[40] More important than discussing life after death is living in the presence of God now. "When life is an answer [to God], death is a homecoming."[41] Further he declares:

> The life that follows must be earned[42] while we are here. It does not come out of nothing; it is an ingathering, the harvest of eternal moments achieved while on earth.
>
> Unless we cultivate sensitivity to the glory while here, unless we learn how to experience a foretaste of heaven while on earth, what can there be in store for us in life to come.[43]

Death is not an event to be feared, nor is it something that one runs to embrace in order to escape a "vale of tears." Rather, we are to live our lives in the here and now world, in partnership with God. When this is done, death is confidently met, because we are living with the One who created both this life and the one to come.

ONCE MORE

In summary, modern Judaism continues to be the religion of Torah. The commandments are her existence. They call Jews to do acts of love and justice. Following the God who reveals himself in Torah means taking a "leap of action" as well as a "leap of faith." Faith must become deed.

God declares his basic trust in humanity in giving the Torah to people. In this act he reveals his need of us in the task of redeeming the world. The gift of the Torah is a call to become partners with God.

Although there is an inclination to evil within us—and too often we succumb to its power—strength to resist this sinful impulse is found in studying and obeying the Torah. When there is failure God responds forgivingly to sincere repentance and welcomes us back to the task he has set before us in the Torah. Judaism recognizes the presence of sin within humankind but does not focus attention on this aspect of life. It chooses to point to the ability of human beings to perform the Torah. God knew our capabilities before giving the Law. He would not command us to do what is beyond us.

Traditionally, Judaism has taken a sober, but optimistic view of this world. This is not a throw-away universe. God has created it and intends it to be a place in which his will is done. Although Jewish tradition treasures the hope of life beyond the grave, there exists little speculation concerning it. Emphasis rests on obeying Torah—on being a responsible partner of God in this life. He himself is responsible for the future.

NOTES

1. Chaim Stern (ed.), *Gates of Prayer: The New Union Prayerbook* (New York: Central Conference of American Rabbis, 1975), p. 438.
2. Lionel Blue, *To Heaven with Scribes and Pharisees: The Jewish Path to God* (New York: Oxford University Press, 1976), p. 17.
3. See the discussion of Eliezer Berkovits, *God, Man and History: A Jewish Interpretation* (New York: Jonathan David, 1959), pp. 87ff.
4. See the various articles on Heschel, contributed by Jewish and Christian scholars, in the magazine *America* (March 10, 1973).
5. Excerpted from GOD IN SEARCH OF MAN by Abraham Joshua Heschel. Copyright © 1955 by Abraham Joshua Heschel. Reprinted with the permission of Farrar, Straus & Giroux, Inc., p. 136.
6. Abraham J. Heschel, *The Prophets* (New York: Harper & Row, 1962), p. 224. See also the comments of Eliezer Berkovits, an orthodox scholar, in *God, Man and History: A Jewish Interpretation.* Although Rabbi Berkovits is critical of Heschel's concept of Pathos, he too discovers the caring God in the revelation of Torah. God is the one

> who reveals Himself by caring involvement in His creation. . . . The essence of the law . . . is an expression of God's continued concern with man. That God commands man is in itself the proof that he does consider him. The law represents the highest affirmation of man, as well as his crowning dignity. By giving man the law, his Maker declares: I do care how he lives and what he does with his life. (P. 87)

7. See our discussion on Law in Chapter Two.
8. "A Conversation with Abraham Joshua Heschel," p. 9. Typescript of a television interview on "The Eternal Light" program. National Broadcasting Company, Inc., 1973.
9. *God in Search of Man,* p. 293.
10. *Ibid.,* p. 306. Cf. p. 309.
11. *Ibid.,* p. 296.
12. *Ibid.,* p. 282.
13. *Ibid.,* p. 282.
14. *Ibid.,* p. 310.
15. *Ibid.,* p. 345.
16. *Ibid.,* pp. 310f.
17. Jim Wallis, *Agenda for Biblical People* (New York: Harper & Row, 1976), p. 29.
18. *God in Search of Man,* p. 326. Cf. also pp. 302 f.
19. Braude, vol. 1, pp. 120-22.
20. Abraham Heschel, *The Insecurity of Freedom* (Philadelphia: Jewish Publication Society, 1966), p. 158.

21. Fritz A. Rothschild, (ed.), *Between God and Man: An Interpretation of Judaism* (New York: The Free Press, 1965), p. 134.
22. Abraham Heschel, *The Insecurity of Freedom,* p. 152.
23. "A Conversation with Abraham Joshua Heschel," p. 4. See also *Between God and Man,* pp. 140-45.
24. *God in Search of Man,* p. 378.
25. Abraham Joshua Heschel, *A Passion for Truth* (New York: Farrar, Straus and Giroux, 1973), p. 253.
26. See 2 Esdras 7:118: "O Adam, what have you done? For though it was you who sinned, the fall was not yours alone, but ours also who are your descendants."
27. *A Passion for Truth,* p. 254.
28. *God in Search of Man,* p. 377.
29. *Ibid.,* p. 379.
30. *Ibid.,* p. 376.
31. *Ibid.,* p. 279.
32. *Ibid.,* p. 375.
33. *Ibid.,* p. 403.
34. *Ibid.,* pp. 402-403.
35. *Ibid.,* p. 378. (Emphasis mine.)
36. *Ibid.,* p. 380.
37. Abraham Joshua Heschel, *The Earth Is the Lord's* (New York: Harper Torch Books, 1966), p. 109. (Published together with *The Sabbath.*)
38. Blackman, Avoth 4:16-17, p. 522 (Order Nezikin).
39. Louis Jacobs, *Faith* (London: Vallentine, Mitchell, 1968), pp. 191-95.
40. "A Conversation with Abraham Joshua Heschel," p. 20.
41. Abraham J. Heschel, "Death as Homecoming," in *Jewish Reflections on Death* edited by Jack Riemer. (New York: Schocken, 1974), p. 73.
42. Christians tend to read legalism into the word "earned." Heschel does not use it in this way. I think he meant that one must be a *responsible* partner with God in this life if the next one is to have any meaning for him. The term "earn" is used also in this same manner by Lionel Blue, *To Heaven with Scribes and Pharisees,* p. 109: "So Jews try to earn their way to heaven, by patching up the world, and making it work."
43. Abraham J. Heschel, "Death as Homecoming," *Jewish Reflections on Death,* p. 72.

FOR FURTHER READING

Berkovits, Eliezer. *God, Man and History: A Jewish Interpretation.* New York: Jonathan David, 1959. A clear presentation of basic elements of Jewish belief by an articulate orthodox scholar. His comments on the ethical and ritual aspects of Torah deserve special attention.

Blue, Lionel. *To Heaven with Scribes and Pharisees: The Path to God.* New

York: Oxford University Press, 1976. A very readable, sometimes humorous, presentation of the "inside" of modern Judaism. Chapter Two, "Earning a Living in the Cosmos," considers the place of Torah in the Jewish tradition.

Neusner, Jacob, (ed.). *The Life of Torah: Readings in Jewish Religious Experience.* Encino, California: Dickenson, 1974. Numerous essays on the nature of Torah in ancient and modern Judaism make this an invaluable volume for the Christian reader.

Rothschild, Fritz A., (ed.). *Between God and Man: An Interpretation of Judaism from the Writings of Abraham Joshua Heschel.* New York: The Free Press, 1965. Paper. Dr. Rothschild has selected passages from *Man Is Not Alone: A Philosophy of Religion* and *God in Search of Man: A Philosophy of Judaism,* both important volumes authored by Heschel. The editor has also written a valuable introduction to the thought of Abraham Heschel. Probably the best way "in" to this influential Jewish thinker.

Sherman, Franklin. *The Promise of Heschel.* New York: J. B. Lippincott, 1970. A very useful guide to Heschel's mind. Provides brief summaries of some of his books and includes a bibliography.

Chapter Ten

A
CHRISTIAN APPROACH
TO JUDAISM

A WORD TO CHRISTIAN INSIDERS

The previous chapters are an attempt to erase the caricature of Judaism that has existed in Christian circles for centuries. They represent an "outsider's" attempt to appreciate some central aspects of Jewish teaching. However, if there is to be genuine dialogue between the Jewish community and the Church, not only must Christians give a fair representation of Judaism, but we must be self-critical of the *manner* in which the Christian message is proclaimed. For this reason, the concluding chapter focuses on Christianity.

ONE THING LEADS TO ANOTHER

"And caricature begat exaggeration." This is what happened often when Christians compared Judaism to Christianity. Not only was a caricature of Judaism drawn, but the achievements of Christianity were exaggerated. This double misrepresentation still prevails, and it hinders true conversation between the two faiths. It prevents us from discovering the actual shapes of Judaism and Christianity, and the places where they really differ. However, the practice of distortion and exaggeration is not a habit peculiar to Christians. It is at home among Jews also. Christianity often takes on a misshapen form in Jewish thought, while Judaism assumes a grandeur not visible to Christians. But, this volume is addressed to Christians; therefore the principal concern is the thinking of the Christian community. The plan of the book does not include a full-scale discussion of the above issue. However, one example of this occurrence of caricature and exaggeration in Christian thought will illustrate the need for serious conversation between Jews and Christians.

CARICATURE

The Christian caricature of Jewish teaching on Law has been a central concern of this volume. It is true that Judaism *is* the Way of Torah; it *is* a religion of Law. Christians have supposed, however, that this emphasis on Law creates a burdensome, legalistic religion. Further, it is said, while the Law itself may be good, it only tells us what we *should* do. It gives no strength to do it. It cannot change the heart so that one would *want* to obey it. Because of this inadequacy, Judaism lacks ability to transform the world. In the period preceding the rise of Christianity, Judaism was in its last phase. It was a tired, formalistic, lifeless legalism, in which one found little hope or joy. The religion of Law proved to be a failure. Such has been the view of Judaism in the minds of many Christians.

EXAGGERATION

Christians declare that into the dark era ruled by Law, came Jesus Christ. He brought with him the good news of hope and life, which is available to people of every age. Those who meet him, and believe in him, become changed persons. They are "in Christ" (2 Cor. 1:21) and have received a "new nature." (Col. 3:10) Jesus Christ has brought about a "new creation; the old has passed away, behold, the new has come." (2 Cor. 5:17) We are no longer under the burdensome Law. We do not live in our own strength but in the power of Christ. Jesus is the Savior and Redeemer of the world. His coming has inaugurated a New Age. He has split the world into B.C. and A.D.

SAYING TOO LITTLE AND TOO MUCH

When we look at Judaism and Christianity in the light of the two preceding paragraphs, Judaism does not appear to be a very appealing religion! On the face of it, the choice seems simple: living in the Old Age under the Law, which only judges us, or living victoriously in the New Age with the strength of Christ. But can we leave it there? Unquestionably, Judaism and Christianity differ significantly on issues relating to faith and life. But is it fair to state the differences as we have done above? Have we not caricatured Judaism and idealized Christianity? Have we not said too little about the character of Jewish faith and too much about the nature of the Christian Community?

THE NEW AGE

The Church celebrates the coming of Christ as that event which separates B.C. from A.D. A new Age has arrived. We live now in *Anno Domini* (A.D.), the year of our Lord. But what exactly is the meaning of this statement? Do we live in an absolutely New Age? How different was life in 6 B.C. from life in 6 A.D.? In practical terms, what happened in the everyday world with the coming of Jesus? Is the world better? Is God's presence in this world more easily discerned than it was before?

In the Old Testament, and in later Jewish thought, the New Age is conceived of as the age in which God rules. During this period, peace, justice, and kindness will reign. How does the coming of Jesus, and the creation of the Church, relate to this hope of the Old Testament? Jews notice that peace, justice, and kindness do not rule now in this world. It may be that the world is worse off today than it was before the coming of Jesus.

Nations have developed hideous weapons of destruction. There has been no cutting back on cruelty and hate. Raw power often rules this world; truth and justice are too frequently on the scaffold. Even among those who profess to follow Jesus Christ, there is disharmony and hostility. Further, the murder of six million Jews took place in what Christians call the New Age. Is it possible for such horrible things to happen in *the* New Age? If the last nineteen hundred years had been a Jewish civilization, and Jews claimed that this period was the New Age, would we agree with them?

TOGETHER WE WAIT

Jews hear the Christian claim that we live in a New Age, but they ask, does it square with the way life actually is? Sins that go back to the earliest civilizations are still with us. This cannot be the New Age, declare Jewish theologians, because it is not new. This cannot be the Age of Redemption, because, as a matter of fact, the world is not redeemed. Jews remind us that even the Christian Church recognizes that the world is not yet redeemed, because we look to the second coming of Jesus. Further, they call attention to the Christian description of Jesus' final coming. It appears to correspond basically to the Old Testament and Jewish hope for the future; that is, it refers to a time when God will reign fully and bring about his will. If Jews and Christians do not hope for the exact same thing, it is, at least, very similar.

NEW AGE, NEW CREATION, NEW NATURE

In the light of these observations, how do we, as Christians, describe the present time in which we now live? How does one respond to Jews, who say that the last 1900 years cannot possibly be the New Age or the Age of Redemption because there is too much of the old and the unredeemed in it? The Apostle

Paul's comments on the significance of Jesus Christ may help us make response to this question. He rejoices that "in Christ" a Christian becomes a "new creation" and takes on a "new nature." At first sight it may appear that Paul is talking about an absolutely new creation. Some Christian preachers seem to interpret these words in this fashion. In Christ, they say, everything becomes different; the old has passed away and the new has come. This kind of preaching has caused severe problems for a good number of earnest Christians, because all things have not become new for them. They are still struggling with the old self and with old sins. In some Christian circles people do not feel free to admit that they have serious personal problems because, it is believed, true Christians should not have these problems. "Do not Christians possess a new nature? Is not the unlimited power of Christ available to us? Should we not be able to overcome personal difficulties?" Such an understanding was, and still is, the basis for some Christian opposition to psychiatrists and counselors. Christians should not have need of these professionals because they have Christ. But the fact is that most, if not all, Christians experience serious personal problems in the living of this life. The power of Christ is available to them, but the inner conflict is real. If only "trouble-free" persons qualify as Christians, then the followers of Christ in this world number less than the original twelve disciples.

IN CHRIST, BUT ALSO IN THE WORLD

In enthusiastic "testimony" language, Paul declares that we are a "new creation," live "in Christ" and "sit with him in the heavenly places." (Eph. 2:6) This is hyperbolic speech; it is the language of preaching. In attempting to describe the wonderful experience he had with Christ, Paul is pushed to use superlative terms. These words are to be taken seriously, but they need to be interpreted by our own experience within the Christian community. The words speak of a revolutionary change that Paul and others experienced in meeting Jesus Christ. But, it is apparent from the New Testament writings that this change was not a complete transformation. Although the early Christians "lived in Christ" and Christ "lived in them," they continued to struggle with temptation; they still committed evil acts. In Paul's letters to various churches, he deals with serious problems that arose among those who had come to Christ: for example, idolatry, dissension, immorality, pride, jealousy, slander, selfishness. Is it possible for people who are "in Christ" to be guilty of these sins?

Paul was a realist. He lived in this world and experienced the same conflicts we all face. He witnesses to Christ's ability to bring about radical change in a person's life, but he also recognizes that this person continues to sin and stands in need of forgiveness. Martin Luther, the great interpreter of Paul, described the situation of the Christian very well when he declared that the Christian is both a saint and a sinner. This dual aspect of the Christian life finds confirmation in the experiences of millions of Christians, who have lived out their lives in the last nineteen hundred years. The Church as an institution manifests this "saint-sinner" character also. It has represented the spirit of Christ in this world, but it has also contributed its share of darkness. Christians are "in Christ" but they are also very much "in" and a part of this world. We possess a "new nature," but, from awareness of our own experiences, as well as those of others, we know that the "old nature" still hangs on. We live in a New Age but the Old Age remains.

CONVEYING INSIDE TRUTH TO OUTSIDE PEOPLE

What we have said above is no brand-new insight to Christians. Most people within the Church recognize that the life of a Christian has a saint-sinner character to it. None of us expects to see a person who is an absolutely "new creation" in Christ. *However, in our preaching and witnessing to people of other faiths, we sometimes convey the idea that Jesus brings about a complete change in our life.* This is often what happens when we compare Judaism and Christianity. In setting Jesus against the Law, we note the powerlessness of the Law while declaring that in Christ we become a new creation, are born anew, or are raised from the dead. In this context we seem to adopt a rather literal understanding of these terms, even though we know that such an understanding does not fit our experience. When we talk about what Christ has done for us, it is only fair to admit to others what we admit to ourselves. We must affirm that Christ effects significant and far-reaching changes in the lives of those who become Christians. But, when we witness of Christ to people outside the Christian community, care must be taken lest we give the impression that Christ transforms us into conflict-free people, or that his coming has brought about a completely New Age. We should not say more about our experience of Christ than our everyday life can support. We need not "improve" on God's work in Jesus Christ in order to make it more attractive.

The existence of the Christian Church reminds us that innumerable people have experienced newness of life through Jesus Christ. In our own day, we are aware of friends and relatives who have found in Christ a way of living that is deeply fulfilling —a way which offers hope in this life and the next. Christ stands at the center of the Christian's relationship to God. However, we need to listen to the realism of the New Testament writings so that we do not idealize the Christian experience and make affirmations that give the wrong impression.

PRELUDE TO AN IMPORTANT QUESTION

Previous chapters in this volume have concentrated on the nature of ancient Israelite faith as well as early and modern

Judaism. The focus has been on Torah and its significance in the Israelite-Jewish tradition. As we have seen, Jews are thankful for the Torah. It is not a dark or burdensome teaching; it is the way of and to life. There have been, of course, extreme persons in Jewish circles who have given a legalistic character to Judaism. But few communities are free of such people. The Christian Church has experienced its own pain and embarrassment with those who make Christianity anything but good news by their excesses in areas of morality and doctrine.

Admittedly, concern for Torah gives Judaism a "personality" that is somewhat different from that of the Christian community. However, though difference exists, there is similarity in some basic beliefs. For example, the commandments of Torah make demands on Jews, but these are the demands of a loving God. Jews do Torah not to earn God's love but to respond to it. When the Law is broken, the righteous and merciful God grants forgiveness to the repentant persons and invites them back to the way of Torah. This is the witness of Judaism, but a Christian finds familiar themes here. Both the Jewish and Christian communities trace their beginnings to and find their nourishment in the grace of God.

As Christians we confess that we are "new creatures" living in a "new age." This is the language of testimony and is to be understood as speech akin to other words of witness. For example, according to the New Testament, we are a people who have been raised from the death of sin and who now sit "in the heavenly places in Christ Jesus." (Eph. 2:5-6) What Paul affirms is true, but, in a very practical sense, it is not true also. In any case it is clear that we are not fully new creatures and we do not live in an absolutely new age. The everyday world is much the same as it always has been. We still struggle with problems experienced by others. Together with Jews we look forward to the time when God will bring his kingdom in fullness and put an end to the conflicts which we find in ourselves.

THE QUESTION: IS JUDAISM A VALID RELIGION?

The old caricatures of Judaism are now recognized as such and are set aside. But, though the record has been set right, it is still true that Judaism is not Christianity and Jews are not Christians. Jews are "outside" of Christ. Does that mean that they are "lost" according to Christian theology? This question touches on a fundamental issue in Jewish-Christian relationships: is Judaism a valid religion? In back of the abstract word "Judaism" stand people—Jewish people. How are we to think about them? Are the great leaders of Judaism false teachers? Have millions of martyred Jews died for an illegitimate faith? Abraham Heschel put the question this way: " 'Do Christians really believe that it is God's will that every synagogue throughout the world be closed?' "[1]

A MISSION TO THE JEWS

The response of the Christian community to these questions has been varied. In addition to a general evangelism effort, some people within the Church have supported a mission to the Jews. They believe that everyone, including the Jews, must come to God through Jesus Christ (John 14:6). The rationale for a special mission to Jewish people rests in Jesus' life and ministry among them—his own people. These Christians see their effort as a continuation of his work.

In recent years the Church's support of Jewish evangelism has diminished. Denominational bodies and individual Christians are reevaluating the legitimacy of such an effort. Some conservative groups have radically revised their relationship to Jewish people. One example is the *Nes Ammim* (Banner of the Peoples) community in Israel. Although this settlement represents conservative Christian thought, its members have determined to "refrain from missionary proselytism, both in practice and in principle." They participate in the life of the Jewish community and seek to be a "sign of solidarity of Christianity with the people of Israel."[2]

JEWS SHOULD BECOME CHRISTIANS BUT . . .

The dominant response in the Church to the question of the validity of Judaism has been the practical one of inaction and noninterference. Persons in this group make the "official" affirmation that "outside of Christ there is no salvation," but, recognizing how few Jews have converted over the centuries, they refrain from any serious effort to convert them. This attitude sometimes surfaces at high levels within the Church. A pastor is asked by a colleague concerning the growth of his congregation. The pastor responds with the observation that the church has grown very little because it is situated in a Jewish community. To this kind of statement the questioner nods his head in understanding. Neither of them expect that Jews will become Christians. If Jews want to convert they will be warmly welcomed, but there is no concentrated plan to evangelize them. It is recognized that Jews are a special problem!

JEWS BELONG TO THE FAMILY

Others within the Church hold that there is no need to evangelize Jews because they are convinced that those who follow the teachings of Judaism are a part of the family of faith. Some who adopt this view, including front-ranking New Testament scholars and church people, believe they are guided to this position by Paul's words in Romans 9–11 which speak about Israel's relationship to God.[3] In addition, a growing number of persons are embarrassed at the negative assessment of Judaism in view of the Church's own long term involvement in injustice and cruelty. For these people it does not seem right to work for the conversion of Jews when the Church itself needs to be turned around. In a recent article, Isaac C. Rottenberg, a prominent minister in the Reformed Church of America announced his withdrawal from any program of Jewish evangelism for the reasons stated above. The Church has no right to missionize the Jews as if it were the superior community. However, the Church can and should, says Rottenberg, enter into a relationship with Jewish people in which witness is given and received. In this kind of relationship both communities may hear God speaking to them.

> Believers who share the covenant faith that has come to us through Moses and the prophets don't missionize each other. Yet there ought to be room for witness, the sharing of faith perspectives and the exchange of deeply held convictions.[4]

THE QUESTION CONCERNS JESUS CHRIST

Ultimately the issue we have been discussing concerns the place of Jesus Christ in the Church and the world. What is our relationship to him? How are we to think of him when we confront Jews? We cannot deny—indeed, we do not wish to deny, that in Jesus Christ we have discerned the presence of God. On the other hand, we do not want to hold to an interpretation of him that is inhumane or out of touch with the experiences of life.

LISTENING TWICE, SPEAKING ONCE

The Christian is tempted to give a quick "doctrinal" answer when considering the relation of Jews to Jesus Christ. At this point in history, it will be wise to exercise restraint and to obey the old proverb "listen twice, speak once." Before an "answer" is formulated we need to know more about who we *really* are and who Jews *really* are. In friendly but serious confrontation with Jews we may gain insights that will help us better understand both Judaism and Christianity. The following words of Hans Küng point the way:

> Only one thing is of any use now: a radical metanoia, repentance and re-thinking; we must start on a new road, no longer leading away from the Jews, but towards them, towards a living dialogue, the aim of which is not the capitulation but simply the understanding of the other side; towards mutual help, which is not part of a "mission", to an encounter in a true brotherly spirit.[5]

To see ourselves as others see us and others as they see themselves has promise for both Jews and Christians. Out of this kind of meeting something new may happen—a newness that we cannot envisage today.

NOTES

1. *Newsweek* (March 19, 1973) p. 59.
2. See information pamphlet issued by the *Nes Ammim* community.
3. See, for example: James D. Smart, *Doorway to a New Age: A Study of Paul's Letter to the Romans* (Philadelphia: Westminster, 1972), pp. 138-46; Krister Stendahl, *Paul Among Jews and Gentiles* (Philadelphia: Fortress Press, 1976), p. 4.
4. Isaac C. Rottenberg, "Should There Be a Christian Witness to the Jews?", *The Christian Century* 94:13 (April 13, 1977) 353. See also his article "The Glory of God and the People of Israel" in the *Reformed World* 34 (1977) 215-21.
5. Hans Küng, *The Church* (New York: Sheed and Ward, 1967), p. 138. See also the comments of Küng in a book he edited with Walter Kasper, *Christians and Jews* (New York: Seabury Press, 1974-75), pp. 12-16.

FOR FURTHER READING

Books by Jewish Authors

Agus, Jacob. *Dialogue and Tradition: The Challenges of Contemporary Judeo-Christian Thought.* New York: Abelard-Schuman, 1971. Some 150 pages of this large book (620 pp.) relates to Jewish-Christian relationships. A fair examination of issues that concern Jews and Christians.

Berkovits, Eliezer. *Faith After the Holocaust.* New York: KTAV, 1973. The author, a Jewish scholar in the Orthodox tradition, while addressing himself to the nature of Jewish faith, gives considerable space to Christianity. Writing against the background of the Holocaust, his remarks often reflect hostility toward the Christian Church. He refers to "the moral bankruptcy of Christian civilization and the spiritual bankruptcy of Christian religion." An important book for Christians to read even though we may feel that some of his statements are unfair.

Bokser, Ben Zion. *Judaism and the Christian Predicament.* New York: Knopf, 1967. An informative, well written book by a professor at Jewish Theological Seminary, New York. Dr. Bokser presents a thorough study of the nature of the Jewish Scriptures, the rabbinic tradition and Christianity in order to isolate the basic issues that Jews and Christians need to discuss together. Although he writes with some passion, his restraint is admirable.

Jacob, Walter. *Christianity Through Jewish Eyes: The Quest for Common Ground.* Cincinnati: Hebrew Union College Press, 1974. Dr. Jacob summarizes and analyzes the views of twenty-one leading Jewish scholars, the earliest of whom lived in the middle seventeen hundreds. His studies of contemporary Jewish writers include such significant figures as: Samuel Sandmel, Richard Rubenstein, Emil Fackenheim, Solomon Zeitlin, and David Flusser. At the end of the volume he offers some conclusions about Jewish-Christian relationships and takes a look at the future.

Sandmel, Samuel. *We Jews and Jesus.* New York: Oxford University Press, 1965. Dr. Sandmel is Professor of Bible and Hellenistic Literature at Hebrew Union College, Jewish Institute of Religion. A Reform Jew, he has given a lifetime of study to Christianity and has been a leader in an attempt to bring about better relationships between Jews and Christians. Of the purpose of this book, Professor Sandmel says: "I have written this little book for those thoughtful Jewish people who seek to arrive at a calm and balanced understanding of where Jews can reasonably stand with respect to Jesus." (P. vii) Christians will find it interesting to read over Jewish shoulders. His last chapter is entitled: "Toward a Jewish Attitude to Christianity."

Talmage, Frank E., (ed.). *Disputation and Dialogue: Readings in the Jewish-Christian Encounter.* New York: KTAV, 1975. An invaluable resource for understanding the two thousand year "disputation and dialogue" between Jews and Christians. Selections include the writings of Jewish and Christian leaders and deal with such subjects as: Anti-Jewishness (ancient and modern), the Messiah, Law and Gospel, the Land of Israel, and the Jewish-Christian dialogue.

Tanenbaum, Marc H., Marvin R. Wilson and James A. Rudin, (eds.). *Evangelicals and Jews in Conversation on Scripture, Theology, and History.* Grand Rapids: Baker, 1978. Essays by Jewish and Evangelical Christian leaders on various topics, including: "The Messiah," "The Meaning of Israel," "Interpretation of Scripture," and "Religious Pluralism."

Weiss-Rosmarin, Trude. *Judaism and Christianity: Their Differences.* New York: Jonathan David Publishers, 1943. The author decided to write this book "because I arrived at the conclusion that it was high time to stress in *Jewish* circles that 'goodwill' between Jews and Christians should not and must not be synonymous with raising all bars and obliterating or denying the differences that separate the two faiths." (P. 7) The polemical style does not lessen the importance of this book for Christians. The author discusses such topics as: God, Miracles, Sin and Atonement, Faith vs. Law, Interpretation of Judaism, and Jesus.

Books by Christian Authors

Davies, Alan T. *Anti-Semitism and the Christian Mind: The Crisis of Conscience After Auschwitz.* New York: Herder and Herder, 1969. Following a brief section devoted to the anti-semitic behavior of the Church, the author reviews the thought of some post-Auschwitz Catholic and Protestant theologians who have struggled with this dark side of Christianity. Among those discussed are: D. Judant, Jacques Maritain, Jean Daniélou, Augustin Bea (Catholic); Karl Barth, Leonhard Ragaz, Reinhold Niebuhr, James Parkes (Protestant).

Eckardt, A. Roy. *Your People, My People: The Meeting of Jews and Christians.* New York: Quadrangle, 1974. Dr. Eckardt, in numerous books and articles has long worked within the Church for a better understanding of Jews and Judaism. Feeling the weight of Auschwitz, he calls Christians to confront and reject the Church's anti-Jewish past. He reviews the past and present relationships between the two faiths and gives considerable space to a discussion of the state of Israel. The final chapter ("Toward Authenticity") attempts to define a "positive, authentic Jewish-Christian relationship." Eckardt's contribution is a highly valued one and deserves the attention of the Christian reader even though the tone of the writing is sometimes unnecessarily sharp and dogmatic.

Fleischner, Eva. *Judaism in German Christian Theology Since 1945: Christianity and Israel Considered in Terms of Mission.* Metuchen, New Jersey: The Scarecrow Press, 1975. An important book which not only describes the present theological scene in Germany but also challenges the reader to ponder the character of the Church's witness in the world.

Fleischner, Eva, (ed.). *Auschwitz: Beginning of a New Era?* New York: KTAV, 1977. Papers given by Jewish and Christian scholars at a conference on the Holocaust held at the Cathedral of Saint John the Divine in New York City in 1974.

Küng, Hans and Walter Kasper, (eds.). *Christians and Jews.* New York: Seabury Press, 1974-75. Essays on themes important to both Judaism and Christianity by well-known scholars. Do not overlook Hans Küng's introduction: "From Anti-Semitism to Theological Dialogue."

Kirsch, Paul J. *We Christians and Jews.* Philadelphia: Fortress Press, 1975. Paper. A brief but informative discussion which covers such topics as: Judaism in the New Testament, the messiahship and death of Jesus, evangelism and the Jew, the Holocaust, and the state of Israel.

Littell, Franklin H. *The Crucifixion of the Jews: The Failure of Christians to Understand the Jewish Experience.* New York: Harper and Row, 1975. No calm essay in this volume! It is a passionate call to the Christian Church to repent of its anti-Jewishness. Among the topics discussed are: Christian anti-semitism, the Church in Germany during the Nazi persecution, the Holocaust and the state of Israel. An appendix offers a Holocaust Liturgy for use in the Christian Church.

Ruether, Rosemary R. *Faith and Fratricide: The Theological Roots of Anti-Semitism.* New York: The Seabury Press, 1974. A readable, thorough study of Jewish-Christian relationships. Special emphasis is given to the conflict reflected in the New Testament and to the anti-Jewishness of the Church Fathers. The author believes that Christian anti-semitism is deeply embedded in Christian theology and that a direct line links the Church's anti-Jewishness and the furnaces of Auschwitz. In the last chapter she suggests a new approach to the Jewish community.